# Wales at War

# Wales at War

## THE EXPERIENCE OF THE
## SECOND WORLD WAR IN WALES

### STUART BROOMFIELD

The
History
Press

First published 2009

The History Press
The Mill, Brimscombe Port
Stroud, Gloucestershire, GL5 2QG
www.thehistorypress.co.uk

British Library Cataloguing in Publication Data.
A catalogue record for this book is available from the British Library.

ISBN 978 0 7524 5190 9

Typesetting and origination by The History Press
Printed in Great Britain

# Contents

# Acknowledgements

This book has been a long time in the making. Thirty years ago I completed a PhD on the South Wales coal industry during the Second World War. In 2002 a chance meeting with Professor Gareth Williams led to the inception of this work with its much wider remit. There are many people whose support has been essential in enabling me to achieve completion.

I am particularly grateful to Dr Keith Strange who generously provided me with an unpublished account of the experiences of evacuation in Cardiff, based on the daily accounts written in school log books. Without this significant contribution the section on evacuation in Chapter One would have been rather sparse.

The contribution of my close work colleague and friend for over twenty-five years, David Maddox, was invaluable, especially in the gathering of the pictorial evidence. Over many years as schools adviser for history in Mid-Glamorgan, and post local government reorganisation in 1996 to the counties of Bridgend, Caerphilly, Merthyr Tydfil and Rhondda Cynon Taf, David has built up a fascinating archive of material on the Second World War which has been disseminated on courses for teachers and projects for children and young people. Through his encouragement other teacher colleagues have produced booklets on various aspects of the wartime period. Foremost amongst these are those produced by Fay Swain, Philip Tapper and Philip again, working with

Susan Hawthorne. I have been able to draw upon their work to enhance my script. David has spent much time identifying suitable photographs to partner the text and I very much appreciate his support. He has a fund of knowledge of the period and having read the manuscript, offered good advice and identified areas to be developed.

Given that the brief for the book was far wider than my original research I have drawn upon a large number of secondary works by dedicated local historians and devotees of particular aspects of wartime experience. I hope that they have been suitably acknowledged within the text. I am grateful, too, to Nevin Williams for the loan of materials related to the air war over Wales.

In 2002 my long time friend, Richard Jones was extremely helpful in researching the story of the storage of the art treasures. To some extent this was superseded by the publication of N.J. McCamley's book. Nevertheless I am very grateful for his efforts and ongoing interest.

I would like to thank Faith Williams for her construction of the index, and the production team at The History Press, led by Simon Hamlet.

Thanks go Media Wales Limited, Llyfrgell Genedlaethol Cymru/ The National Library of Wales, The Glamorgan Record Office, David Maddox, the family of the late Vernon Scott and Mrs Joan Watts for permission to reproduce the illustrations that accompany the text.

Finally I would like to acknowledge family and friends for their support throughout the whole process. I would like to make special mention of Dic Felstead, who has heard much of the detail of the book on our regular Sunday walks, and, of course, my wife Mary for her great tolerance.

# Introduction

One winter evening in the mid-1970s I met the historian, Professor Gwyn Williams, in a public house near Cardiff University. I had heard Gwyn lecture, in his distinctive style, on a number of occasions but had never had a conversation with him. That evening he enquired about the research that I was undertaking into the South Wales coalfield during the Second World War, a period, of course, with which Gwyn had first-hand experience.

I spoke to him about the industrial unrest within the coalfield during the period 1942–1944 that culminated in a complete stoppage of work in March 1944, just three months prior to the D-Day landings. Explanation of this apparent conflict of interest was a topic that was exercising my mind at this time. Gwyn, a great raconteur, took over at this point and told me the following story. This is how I remember what he told me.

It was September 1939. Gwyn, in his mid-teenage years, was at the Urdd summer camp at Llangranog. One evening, Gwyn and his friends got around to talking about sex. As in any group there is always one that professes greater knowledge and experience. This character brought the topic of venereal disease into the conversation. It was possible, he said, to contract the disease from lavatory seats. He knew of a test that they could take to find out whether they had the disease or not. They should take a penny and press it against the end of their 'John Willy'. If it burned you had VD, if not you were okay. Gwyn found himself a penny, hid behind a hedge and undertook the test. To his horror, he diagnosed himself as having VD!

A sleepless night followed. Early next morning, however, there was more dramatic news. Adolf Hitler had invaded Poland. The camp was to be broken up early and the boys were to return home to Merthyr. On the journey back Gwyn knew the seriousness of the international situation but his great fear was about how he was going to tell his mother that he had caught VD.

Incisive, as ever, Gwyn had got to the nub of the issue. There is often a conflict between what should be done for the greater good and what are one's personal hopes and concerns. As we look back over sixty years or more from an age in which programmes on the Second World War appear daily on multi-channel television, there is an impression that individuals living through those momentous events would be consumed by their involvement. The reality is that for those on the Home Front the events of the war were an integral backcloth to their lives, but each and every person had their own independent existence in which their feelings and actions were fashioned by personal experiences in the home, at school, in the workplace and in the wider community. Epitomising this is the work of documentary novelist Bert Coombes, a miner-writer, who lived in Resolven in the Neath Valley. He had two short works published during the Second World War, *Those Clouded Hills* and *Miners Day*. They are largely about conditions of working in the colliery during wartime and are almost exclusively about pit matters. Only those events that impinged upon a miner's work are discussed and wider aspects of the war and details of events are very much in the background.

For many the war was a stimulus to debate a wider vision for humanity in a post-war world but for others there were simple and limited hopes concerned with their own future economic security in a more hospitable environment. Author, Susan Briggs in her book *Keep Smiling Through: The Home Front 1939–1945* suggests that

> For some intellectuals from the very beginning, they had had dreams of Europe. For most people, however, they were dreams not even of Britain, but of Exeter, Leeds, or Selkirk … and particular streets and particular people in them … localised dreams centring on particular jobs, homes, towns and villages.

Gwyn Williams passed away in 1995 after a long struggle with illness. Shortly after his death a booklet, *Fishers of Men — Stories towards an Autobiography* was published. It is a collection of autobiographical stories. Amongst the stories is one entitled 'Welsh and a Social Disease'. It is the story of Gwyn's last day at the Urdd camp in Llangrannog. Its telling is far more entertaining and detailed than the version above and it differs in another respect.

> … I had VD! … I never slept all night … How was I going to tell Mam? Tell her that I had VD …
>
> But in the morning, a Friday, Hitler did indeed go into Poland … and I forgot about my VD.

It is a reminder that the point of a story may be more relevant than the story itself. Most of the stories in *Fishers of Men* are about Gwyn's experiences in the Second World War between the D-Day landings and his demobilisation in 1947. Those experiences clearly made a significant impact upon his psyche. For historians of the Second World War there are untold riches of anecdotal and incidental evidence captured in the memories of those who lived through the period. Indeed, many are still being recorded today, especially with the advent of the internet. Angus Calder, whose momentous work, *The People's War — Britain 1939–1945*, first published in 1969, is still very much the definitive account of the Home Front during the conflict, warns in a later essay that 'memory does not deliver fact … The historian's function is to get behind memory'. Memories do, however, provide a vast range of stories that enable us to evoke the mood of the times and very often provide a 'hook' of interest that encourages one to delve much further.

Drawing together a narrative about the Second World War is a fascinating challenge. Television has popularised the period and in particular because programmers have been able to intersperse commentary with interviews of participants. Few historical studies of periods and topics prior to the war have used oral testimony so extensively, including those of the 'ordinary' people giving their recollections of daily life during the period and the impact on their personal lives. There are rich seams of evidence that enhance the telling of the historical story. BBC research projects, websites and many booklets on individual topics such as evacuees and Yanks provide a goldmine of evidence that can be used to illustrate substantive points and make them more interesting.

On the other hand the volume of evidence can make the creation of the 'big picture' more complex, given the awareness that the testimony of some individuals and communities may be at odds with the general overview. As far as Wales is concerned a significant overview of the Second World War years has not yet been created. Prominent historians such as John Davies and Kenneth Morgan have produced very useful and informative chapters within the context of more substantial works, and specialist, local and amateur historians have produced a range of invaluable books on particular themes, topics and localities. To these can be added chapters from biographies and autobiographies and many short articles in magazines and journals.

In this book an attempt will be made to knit together the individual experiences of people from across Wales against a background of the narrative of the war at home and abroad, whilst at the same time addressing significant themes and events. In writing any history the author has the advantage of hindsight, the knowledge of what happened as a result of events, both in the short term and in the long term. During the war years the most dramatic of domestic political events was the emergence of Winston Churchill as leader of the Conservative Party and the creation of a coalition government in May 1940. Five years later, within months of the end of the war, the great 'war leader', voted the greatest Briton of all time by a BBC television poll in 2004, was ousted from power. The electorate might appear ungrateful if the war years are seen in isolation as the period between September 1939 and May 1945. Any understanding of this dramatic turnabout can only be reached by having knowledge of the psyche of the British people at the time that they entered the war. Events and developments in the war years contributed to the mood of the people but the historical experience of the inter-war years was as significant in its impact.

Whilst being a distinctive period worthy of special study, in domestic history the war years may be seen by some as being mainly a period of dislocation between the depression years and the new, post-war world of the welfare state. Many of the decisions made during the war years were responses to attitudes forged in the past or by hopes for the future. From the middle years of the war, late 1942 and early 1943, the war aims of the people began to take on a domestic hue. Beating Hitler had the further purpose of presenting an opportunity to put into practice some cherished ideals. This process was galvanised by the Beveridge Report, the government commissioned investigation into social conditions. Whilst some had ideals to look forward to, others viewed the end of the war with trepidation. Collective memory, especially in industrial areas like the coalfields of North and South Wales, recalled that economic slump, job insecurity and social hardship followed the First World War. In the light of that past experience there was a desire to ensure that any improvement in wages during the war should be sustained thereafter. Both these attitudes towards the future were moulded in the pre-war years rather than during the war itself.

The war years, however, were a distinctive and unique phase in our history with features that could only be a product of the circumstances that involved both defensive actions designed to protect the lives and livelihoods of the population at times of attack and threatened invasion, and the support for military offensives in air, at sea and on land across the globe. For most of the period – with the exception of the autumn and winter of 1940/1941 – there was a return to virtual full employment. The spectre of unemployment that had haunted families throughout South Wales for a generation was removed. Yet the benefits that might have accrued from such a situation were substantially eroded by the creation of other spectres generated by the war. Most families had relations or friends fighting in the armed services and the tension this brought is beyond measure. The fear of air raid attacks was ever present at certain periods and in the coastal cities of Newport, Cardiff and Swansea those fears became tragic reality. Associated with this were the defensive precautions, not only those associated with protection against air raids but also measures to protect against invasion. In this respect there was a role for Wales that stemmed from its geographical location. Location was also an important factor that saw Wales being used for preparations for offensive action, for example the training of pilots in Snowdonia and of soldiers in the Brecon Beacons.

Living and social conditions were subject to change because of the exigencies of war. Food, clothing and travel were affected by rationing, and perhaps most significantly women's roles changed as they began to work outside the home on a scale hitherto unknown. There was also an influx of people entering the country due to the requirements of war – evacuees, transplanted civil servants, the 'Bevin Boys' who worked in the collieries, the American GIs, refugees and prisoners of war.

A feature of wartime is the feats of individuals undertaking actions that in times of peace would not be expected of them. The lives of the young men and women who left Wales as part of the armed forces were changed forever. For many, enduring the privations of military life and engaging in battle was courageous in itself, whilst others undertook actions that were exceptional in their heroism. Such heroism was not confined to the military and there are many civilian stories from the Home Front that merit acknowledgement. War creates its own stories that are often more interesting than the sum of the parts. An assessment of the overall impact of the war on Welsh society may appear dry in comparison. It is the aim in this book, however, to attempt to marry these two elements.

# Chapter One

# The Strategic Position of Wales – Munitions, Military Training, Evacuees and Works of Art

## Pre-war Wales

The 'Hungry Thirties' and the 'Devil's Decade' are just two of the nomenclatures given to the years of economic depression that were drawing to a close shortly before the start of the Second World War. These phrases conjure up images of cloth-capped unemployed men standing on street corners, hunger marches and industrial conflict. Wales was very much at the centre of the Depression and a large part was officially designated a 'distressed area'.

There are some historians that consider these images to be a distortion of the true picture, as the Depression was felt to differing degrees in different parts of Britain. Some parts witnessed an increase in prosperity. Light engineering industry prospered in south-east England and the motor car industry in the Midlands. Workers there benefited from an increase in real wages, shorter hours and longer holidays. Prosperity was reflected in the ownership of items such as radios and electrical appliances. The professional classes could show off their affluence by possession of one of the million cars sold in these years and the purchase of one of the four million new homes that were built.

There were isolated places in Wales where prosperity was clearly on show. Many of the new houses were built in 'suburbia' on the outskirts of large towns. Both Cardiff and Swansea, for example, still have many good examples of houses built in the 1930s – houses with mock-Tudor timbers, leaded window frames and large gardens with room for a garage and garden shed. Along the coast of North Wales towns such as Rhyl, Prestatyn, Llandudno, Bangor and Caernarfon benefited from the beginnings of a tourist boom and their desirability as locations for retirement homes. The world of the affluent people who retired in the new luxury houses that lined the Menai Straits, Conwy and Criccieth was, however, a very different one to that of families displaced from the slate quarrying villages a few miles away. Deprivation brushed shoulders with privilege.

Throughout the whole of Wales both industrial and agricultural decline had an impact on people's livelihoods and significantly, for the future, their attitudes and beliefs. Nearly a quarter of Welsh males worked in the coal industry. Its decline in the 1920s and 1930s had a widespread impact across Wales but especially the coalfield area in South Wales stretching from Newport and Pontypool in the east to the Gwendraeth and Tawe valleys in the west, and parts of Denbighshire and Flintshire in north-east Wales. Coalfield villages suffered mass unemployment with consequent human suffering and serious industrial dispute and strife.

The coal industry was not alone in its declining fortune. The iron and steel industry, hard hit by competition from Germany and the US, saw the closing down of works in Merthyr, once the cradle of the iron industry, Blaenavon, Tredegar and Ebbw Vale. Welsh tinplate suffered too, in Llanelli and the Amman Valley. In North Wales the slate quarrymen became victims of unemployment as production costs increased and demand fell back due to competition from tiles as a roofing material. By 1938 only one Welsh home in five was roofed with Welsh slate. Decline in industry affected the ports. In 1937 Caernarfon saw its last export of slate. The docks in Cardiff and Barry – the main exporters of Welsh coal – suffered worst.

In many areas where industry declined, there was no alternative employment. A chain reaction set in and shops and service industries were affected too. Empty, derelict buildings, the remains of factories and other business became features of many a town and village.

Rural Wales did not escape. The woollen industry struggled to survive. Of 151 working mills in 1922, just seventy-seven were operative in 1939. The 1930s saw Welsh agriculture in serious difficulties. Farming income fell and farmers facing hardship tended to rely on the family unit to do the work, which meant that there was less work for farm labourers who were forced to leave the countryside and go elsewhere in search of a job. This in turn led to depopulation in rural areas as many joined the half a million people who left the country between 1921 and 1939 to live and work in England or further afield.

In November 1918, Lloyd George had stirred up the hopes for the future at the end of the First World War. 'Don't let us waste this victory merely by ringing bells of joy. This must be a land fit for heroes to live in' was his famous slogan. It was a promise quickly broken as post-war dreams quickly turned sour. The failed promise and the chastening reality of post-war experience for the majority of the population remained in their consciousness throughout the Second World War.

The government was slow to respond to the crisis of industrial decline and unemployment in Wales and elsewhere. In 1933, a committee of enquiry was held into industrial conditions in certain 'depressed areas'. The picture painted of Wales was especially bleak. In the eastern part of the South Wales coalfield between the Rhondda Valleys and Pontypool, unemployment was 44.5 per cent. A high proportion of these people had been without work for over five years.

In 1934, partly as a result of the enquiry report, four 'special' or 'distressed' areas were established, including one in Wales – western Monmouthshire and most of Glamorgan, excluding Cardiff, Barry and Swansea. Each 'special area' was allocated £1 million to provide financial assistance to employers and firms wishing to set up business there. Possibly due to the poor image that prospective employers had of the South Wales 'special area', no new factories were set up until 1938. That year saw another government initiative being applied to Wales when a trading estate opened at Treforest, near Pontypridd. By the end of 1939 between sixty and seventy firms were in operation there. Many of these were owned by refugees from Germany and Austria, fleeing from Nazi oppression. 1938 also saw major developments in the steel industry with the opening of a new strip mill at Ebbw Vale and a sheet making plant at Shotton in Flintshire.

From 1938 unemployment in Wales began to fall. The background to this recovery, however, was in itself no cause for celebration. Grim political reality had finally persuaded the government of the need to respond to the mounting military might of Nazi Germany. The true impact of the rearmament programme began to show itself in 1939. Between March and September 1939 there were 56,000 new jobs in Wales. In the end it was war that provided the boost that would bring Wales back to almost full employment. As well as bringing new industries to the region, the old staple industries also benefited. Coal in particular was a vital commodity and Wales was crucial in supplying Britain's hard-pressed ally, France. In January 1940, the *Western Mail* wrote: 'Not since the last war has there been such a prospect of maximum employment, increasing output, high wages, and reasonable profits.'

Rearmament had been the focus of heated political debate throughout the 1930s. In the early part of the decade the government had placed its hopes in the League of Nations as an effective arbiter between countries to achieve international disarmament. The belligerence of Hitler had changed attitudes and rearmament became an official policy in 1935. The focus was primarily upon the air force, in recognition of the potential importance of aerial bombing if war broke out, especially since Hitler was already building up his air force to a level greater than that of Britain. Another thrust after 1936 was the decision to expand the arms industry and as a result to build new Royal Ordnance Factories and private arms factories. Progress was relatively slow until 1938. Acceleration followed the crisis over the Nazi annexation of Czechoslovakia in September 1938.

The expectation that aerial bombardment would play a significant role in any attack on Britain was critical for Wales. On the western side of Britain it could be considered to be an area that was less likely to feel the brunt of Nazi attacks. Strategically it was a good location for factories and businesses.

## War Industry

The initial focus of government rearmament plans was the air force, and Wales with its western location was integral to the production of aircraft and aircraft weaponry and to air force training schemes. Gwynedd in the north-west, for example, was to witness the building of seven military airfields in the early years of the war. Further east at Broughton the government had selected a site in November 1937 for the building of a factory to build large numbers of aircraft in the case of hostilities. The factory, managed by Vickers-Armstrong, received its first contract for 750 Wellington bombers in May 1939 when the declaration of war was appearing more certain. The test flight of the first plane off the production line took place on 2 August 1939. The total wartime production was to be 5,540 aeroplanes. Over 6,000 workers were employed – half of them women. The factory was featured in a propaganda film that showed the building of a Wellington bomber in twenty-four hours. Close to the factory was the RAF Hawarden airfield where the aircraft had radio and other specialist equipment fitted in readiness for service with the RAF.

Broughton was a purpose built factory, but in other parts of Wales factories were converted to meet aircraft production needs. In South Wales the Ministry of Air Production requisitioned twenty-four of the factories on the new Treforest Trading Estate and at Waunarlwydd, near Swansea, 2,000 workers produced sheet and strip aluminium for aircraft.

Wartime events led to more industries moving from England into Wales. On 15 August 1940 the Hunting Aviation factory at Croydon was so badly damaged following an air raid that production was brought to a halt. The aged David Lloyd George, wartime leader from the First World War, was a friend of the company chairman, Sir Percy Hunting, who was keen to find a permanent location in a 'safe' area. Lloyd George for his part was keen to provide a boost to the local economy. Hunting travelled to Caernarvon to meet Lloyd George and the local MP Goronwy Owen. Two sites, one on the outskirts of Caernarvon and Dinorwig Slate Quarry were chosen and taken over by the company at the end of the month. The pace of events was remarkable. Within two years a workforce of 3,000 was building components for a range of major aircraft. The company changed its name to Necaco Ltd. – the North East Coast Aircraft Company. Given the location in north-west Wales this may seem rather odd. Evidently Sir Percy thought it would mislead German intelligence and thus stop his factory being bombed a second time.

Following the bombing of Coventry the Daimler Company, which produced aero-engine components, moved to Bangor and employed up to 1,000 more workers. On the other side of the Menai Straits the firm of Saunders-Roe relocated from Cowes, the Isle of Wight to Beaumaris.

The work in Beaumaris was to convert American-built flying boats, called Catalinas, to meet RAF operational requirements. Changes had to be made to radio sets, instrumentation and bomb racks. The flying boats were used for anti-submarine patrols and were desperately needed by January 1941. Over 300 were to be converted between 1941 and 1945 and they made a major contribution during the Battle of the Atlantic. Pembroke Dock was the main base for the Catalinas and the Sunderland Flying Boat. They patrolled the Bay of Biscay, hunting for and destroying German U-Boats, and rescuing Allied seamen, victims of U-Boat and aerial attacks.

In addition to the manufacture of equipment for the RAF, sites in Wales were used for the storage of bombs and other resources. In August 1939 the Air Ministry acquired the disused Glynrhonwy Isaf slate quarry near Llanberis, which had closed in 1930. It was considered suitable for the storage of 18,000 tons of bombs. Overhead protection for the quarry was created using broken slate to a depth of forty feet. In January 1942, however, disaster was to strike when two-thirds of the structure collapsed and a train with twenty-seven wagons, in the process of unloading, was engulfed. 14,000 tons of bombs were buried – 14 per cent of the total RAF stock. Most were recovered but no ammunition could be stored at Llanberis again.

In the south-west the RAF had a reserve depot for aviation fuel. A network of fuel tanks was built into the hills north of Milford Haven. In the same area at Trecwm, near Fishguard, the Royal Navy had an armaments depot that it had commandeered in 1938. It was primarily a storage and distribution depot for naval mines but also handled all types of naval munitions and RAF missiles. Trecwn consisted of fifty-eight storage chambers, which extended 200 feet into the hillside. Each chamber had alarmed steel doors and was reached down a siding from a narrow gauge railway. At Caerwent in Monmouthshire a Royal Navy propellant factory was established. Commissioned in 1937, it became fully operational during 1941, employing 2,000 people in the production of cordite.

By far the most significant development in support of the British war machine was the building of royal ordnance factories. Explosives were manufactured at Pembrey in the west and Marchwiel, near Wrexham, whilst at Glascoed, near Pontypool, Bridgend and Rhyd-y-mwyn in north-east Wales the explosives were filled into shells. The shell castings were made at engineering works at Llanishen in the north of Cardiff and Newport. A factory at Hirwaun in the north of Glamorgan produced small arms. In Cardiff 13,000 were employed at Curran's factory making cartridge cases and tracks for tanks.

The shell-filling factories were huge concerns. The Bridgend factory came to employ 35,000 people and the factory at Glascoed, 20,000. The small arms factory at Hirwaun employed 14,000 people. The workforces of these factories were overwhelmingly female. In this respect war was to transform the lives of thousands of women, the lives of their families and the attitudes to and expectations of women in general.

In North Wales the complex at Marchwiel – built in 1940 – was five-miles square and covered 1,400 acres and had its own railway station. It came into production in February 1941 and employed 13,000 people from a radius of 40 miles. The factories were built in such a way that if there was an explosion, damage would be confined to a particular area so that it would not cause overall disruption.

As well as purpose built factories for war production, many existing factories were converted to make goods and equipment required for war. This process began in 1938 when the government assumed powers to direct industries to manufacture 'essential' goods. A factory produced barrage balloons in Cardiff, a sewing machine factory was converted to make magnets and a telephone factory was converted to make light engineering components. Welsh firms all over the country won substantial wartime contracts; in Chepstow the ship building industry – which had closed down in the 1920s – was revived with the construction of tank landing craft that were to be so important for the invasion of France in 1944.

In some cases highly secretive work was carried out in the factories and the workers themselves did not know what it was they were producing. This was the case at Conway where prototypes for the Mulberry harbours – used in the Normandy landings – were developed. An area of the town known as the Morfa was transformed into a huge building site which employed nearly 1,000 men between 1942 and the end of 1944. Further east even more secretive activities were taking place at Rhydymwyn, near Mold. Soon after the outbreak of the war a factory was built for the manufacture of poison gas and in 1942 a sister installation was built. This was an isotope separation plant that was part of Britain's effort to construct an atomic bomb. Local inhabitants were under the impression that the plant manufactured synthetic rubber.

Unemployment, the scourge of the Depression years, was virtually swept away during the Second World War. Nearly 146,000 people were unemployed in 1939; by 1944 this figure was down to just over 7,000. Of those who were employed 55 per cent were serving the war machine, 22 per cent in the armed forces and 33 per cent in civilian employment associated with the war. The nature of work had diversified too. Although large numbers were still working in the old staple industries such as coal and steel, other workers were developing skills in light engineering and manufacturing.

The virtual disappearance of unemployment did not remove the attitudes that were forged during the Depression. Wartime industry was not a permanent solution to the problems that had affected the country in peacetime, and fear of post-war unemployment was to become a significant factor in the formation of attitudes in the closing years of the war.

As well as industry, Wales also became the location for the transference of government departments. The Inland Revenue, for example, moved to Llandudno, the Ministry of Food to Colwyn Bay and the Ministry of Works (ancient monuments) to Rhyl. Within the Ministry of Food there was a section of MI5 operating undercover. It has since become known that their headquarters were in the now demolished Melfort Hotel in Rhos-on-Sea. Many of the hotels in the North Wales coastal towns were taken over by civil servants and their families.

Another white collar group that was evacuated to the country was the light entertainment department of the BBC which found itself based in Bangor. Locals became used to seeing a lot of 'bohemian, artistic types' wandering around the town, including many familiar radio performers. Famous programmes broadcast from Bangor included *ITMA* (*It's That Man Again*), the comedy hit of the war starring Tommy Handley, *Ray's A Laugh*, starring Ted Ray and the BBC Theatre Organ with organist Sandy McPherson who lived in Llandudno. As well as making programmes with the famous names of BBC light entertainment, choirs and local artists from the region were busy making programmes in both Welsh and English for the armed services. Undoubtedly, north-west Wales had a central role in boosting the morale of the people of Britain and the troops abroad.

## Military Training

In 1936 the RAF Bombing School at Penrhos on the Lleyn Peninsula became the centre of national interest when three Welsh Nationalists attempted to burn down buildings there in protest for both pacifist and nationalist reasons. Within five years, however, there were six more airfields in the Gwynedd area. The training of air-gunners, bomb-aimers, navigators and other military personnel at the airfields was a vital cog in the British war machine. Three more airfields were also built in northeast Wales. Aviation activity was to reach an unprecedented high level across North and mid Wales. The region was to play a major role in the training of air crews throughout the war years and they played a critical role in the defence of Britain from air attack in the early years of the war and a major strategic role in the offensive against Germany and its occupied territories during the second half of the war. Similarly South Wales had a major part to play; the largest training base of all was at St Athan in the Vale of Glamorgan which was opened in September 1938. At its peak of operations there were 14,000 personnel working there. Throughout the war 22,000 flight engineers were trained, plus thousands of others such as ground mechanics, wireless and radar operators, physical training instructors and navigators. St Athan was purpose built for training and its buildings included a cinema, a heated swimming pool (the first in Wales), a huge gymnasium and an indoor drill hall.

It was becoming clear by 1938, that there would be a need for the RAF to expand rapidly in terms of machinery, personnel and training operations. New airfields would be necessary to meet the needs. Northwest Britain, including North Wales, was identified as a suitable area for training because it was well away from the predicted area of enemy activity. The mountainous nature of the region had its drawbacks as it limited operational flying, but it was a good training area for navigators and the coastal strips were suitable for bomb-aiming and air-gunnery schools. Pembrokeshire, in south-west Wales was also well placed. Eight airfields were built in the area between 1939–1945.

Throughout the war thousands of aircrews were to be trained. They came, not only from the RAF, but from Australia, New Zealand, South Africa and Canada, the USAAF and from the air forces of occupied countries such as Poland and Czechoslovakia. A visit to the cemetery in Carew Cheriton, near Pembroke brings home the multi-national dimension of this aspect of the war effort. Of the fifteen aircraftmen buried there, four are Canadian, four are Dutch, three are British, two are Polish and one is a New Zealander.

Training was pushed through at as rapid a rate as possible. At RAF Sealand, for example, pilots underwent a sixteen-week course in which they had to complete 100 hours of flying time. At RAF Hawarden, at the height of the Battle of Britain, pilots were given a two-week intensive course on flying Spitfires.

The role of Bomber Command in defeating the German attacks in the late summer and early autumn of 1940 was to be instrumental in preventing the planned Nazi invasion. Throughout the war more than 55,000 air crewmen were to lose their lives – a seventh, over 8,000 men, were to do so in operational training. Ruabon Mountain and the Berwyn Range of mountains to the east, Snowdonia in the north-west and the Brecon Beacons and Black Mountains in central Wales, sadly, had a part to play in this tragic story. In Gwynedd alone, according to Roy Sloan, author of *Wings of War over Gwynedd* some 200 aircrew lost their lives. There were, of course, many more injuries and many planes were damaged or destroyed.

In Snowdonia the majority of crashes were due to aircraft flying into mountains at night or in cloud. Inexperienced aircrews got into difficulties through navigational errors or as a result of technical malfunctions. Pilots of single-seat fighter planes such as the Spitfire or the Mustang, found themselves in charge of high performance machines for the first time. Some in sheer exuberance tried manoeuvres such as diving at high speed and paid with their lives. Training for aerial warfare was hazardous, especially for pilots only recently introduced to high speed aircraft and many collisions took place, often with fatal consequences. A further cause of accidents was a whole range of mechanical failures, unsurprising given the high performance nature of the machinery being stretched to the limits of capability.

Many of the crashes took place on remote hillsides, but there were occasions when civilians on the ground were endangered. Roy Sloan, in his book *Anglesey Air Accidents*, records the tragic death of Dr Mark Chill, his wife and mother-in-law on 19 July 1943. Dr Chill was a medical practitioner who ran a large rural practice from his house in Bodedern. He was on his way to visit patients in the village of Llanddeusant when his car was showered with burning debris. It was set alight and fatal burns were inflicted on those inside. A Vickers Wellington bomber, engaged in a training exercise had suffered double engine failure. Abandoned by its crew, one of whom died when his parachute did not function, the bomber crashed to earth. Roy Sloan describes the accident as being a million to one chance.

Civilians died, too, in attempting to rescue pilots involved in crashes. Roy Sloan provides an account of the tragic event that took place in Anglesey on 28 August 1941. A plane flown by a Polish crew took off from RAF Valley in bad weather and ditched into the sea near Rhosneigr. Two of the crew of three were swept away by heavy seas and the third clung on to the aircraft. Two seventeen-year-old boys launched a dinghy. Showing amazing courage they rowed out to the aircraft. After forty-five minutes they were almost alongside the aircraft when the dinghy capsized. They swam to the aircraft and joined the Polish aviator. They persuaded him to join them in trying to swim back to their dinghy which was being driven back in-shore. He was slightly injured and had to be supported by them. They were able to reach the dinghy and use it for support. They reached a beach defence post which the Pole held on to. He was so exhausted, however, that he lost his grip and was swept away. The boys had struck off to the shore and were rescued themselves by a human chain of soldiers who had gathered on Rhosneigr beach.

Meanwhile, another rescue attempt had been made. Nine men, seven soldiers, a merchant seaman and a local policeman had put out in a whaler to reach the aircraft. It too, capsized and six of the men drowned. Yet another boat manned by a coastguard and an airman put out and it also capsized with the coastguard drowning. An attempt was then made to rescue the rescuers and a group of fourteen soldiers and sailors swam out to rescue those still struggling in the water. Four of this group were also drowned. Altogether there were fourteen deaths, the three airmen and eleven rescuers. The two seventeen-year-olds received the George Medal and the RNLI silver medal.

Wales was also a designated area for infantry training. At the beginning of the war the War Office needed extra land and facilities for this purpose. By the end of the war 200,000 hectares of Welsh land, 10 per cent of the surface of the country, was held by the War Office. Wales became an important area for military training, not only for British battalions, but in the year prior to D-Day for American troops and soldiers from the Commonwealth. Tracts of land became out of bounds for ordinary citizens as soldiers undertook exercises and familiarised themselves with their equipment on firing ranges. In one case, this desire to appropriate land led to a long established community being callously uprooted.

The War Office required an area, at least three miles long, which could be used for artillery practise. Two neighbouring mountains in Breconshire, Mynydd Epynt and Mynydd Bwlch-y-groes, were selected. The area was home to a community of farmers and their families. Fifty-four dwellings had to be evacuated and 219 people were obliged to leave. The eviction was undertaken in an authoritarian manner and no attempt was made to consult the local people. War Office officials visited the area in September 1939 but no further communication was made until March 1940 when all property owners were given one month's notice. No assistance was offered to help them find alternative accommodation, to move or to find alternative employment. There was no significant protest organised. The County Council quickly bowed to the inevitable and the Farmers' Union, whilst also accepting the inevitability of the move, did give help in obtaining compensation. There was some support from the Welsh language press, the Presbyterian Church and the Council for Defence of Welsh Culture, which included members of the Welsh Nationalist Party. Following a visit to London the inhabitants were granted a further month in which to make the move.

The Sennybridge Training Area was the third largest training area in Britain. In addition to the firing ranges for artillery practise, the 29,000-acre site provided tough training for infantry in realistic conditions. Areas of North Wales, too, provided similar terrain for military exercises. The buildings along the promenade of the west coast town of Tywyn, for example, were taken over by the army and there were eight large camps around the town. As with the air force training it was not just the British Army that came to Wales. There were soldiers from the Commonwealth countries, the Americans later in the war and soldiers from countries under Nazi occupation. Amongst the most exotic of visitors training were the Indian transport companies with their mules and horses. They were based in the area around Llafrothen, in north-west Wales for three months in 1942, having previously been in the Crickhowell area close to the Brecon Beacons. Here, a number died in a flu epidemic and they are remembered on gravestones in the local cemetery. In the build up to the Normandy landings parts of Wales were of great importance in the preparations and at one point, there were up to 100,000 troops engaged in exercises.

## Evacuees

Monday 26 April 1937 was a dark day in the annals of European history, made unforgettable for time immemorial by the work of Pablo Picasso. His painting, 'Guernica', is a powerful protest against the horrors of war. What is unique about the painting is that it represents repulsion against a new form of warfare – air attack. The people of the Basque town of Guernica were going about their daily business on market day when German bomber planes, in support of the Spanish fascist leader, General Franco, launched a three-hour attack on the town. Incendiary bombs and high explosives rained down on the population and as the fighter planes plunged low over the centre of the town, machine-guns were fired at those in flight from the terror. The massacre at Guernica was the first strategically planned air raid designed to destroy a European town and terrorise the civilian population.

The British government held the belief from the early 1930s that if Britain were to be involved in another European conflict, air power would be the main instrument of warfare. Experts believed that there would be mass destruction of cities and towns in the first weeks of war with very high death rates. The government issued instructions to local authorities as early as 1935 inviting them to take responsibility for developing 'Air Raid Precautions' to protect their people. The Air Raid Wardens Service was created in April 1937 and training in anti-gas measures for police and local authority workers began. The fears of government were publicised and were often promoted in the press. The attack on Guernica and the later bombings of Barcelona served to emphasise the nature of a future war.

The story of Guernica had a special resonance in many parts of Wales. Volunteers from across the country, but especially from the coalfields had gone out to Spain to fight for the Republican cause against General Franco. Spanish Aid committees that raised funds for the Republican victims of the civil war were a common feature in many communities. Shortly after the bombing of Guernica, the British government provided a ship and naval escort for 4,000 Basque refugee children to come to Britain. Many were to find their way to Wales. Settlements were established in Caerleon in Monmouthshire, Swansea, Brechfa in Carmarthenshire and Old Colwyn near Colwyn Bay. The Basque children became well known across the country. The boys' football team played in many villages and the children were invited to social events.

As part of the government's preparations for the likelihood of air attack it had drawn up plans for evacuation. The country was divided into three types of area – those in danger of attack, which were mainly the major urban centres such as London, Birmingham, Liverpool and Manchester; neutral areas, which were neither to send out evacuees nor were they to become safe or reception areas; and reception areas. The whole of Wales was designated a reception area. The assumption was that Wales was too far to the west to suffer from German bombing raids. In 1939 this was probably a fair judgement to make.

It was an assumption that many thousands of individuals had already arrived at and acted upon. Following the Munich Crisis there was a steady drift back to Wales of people described by John Davies as 'the offspring of London milk retailers sent to the homes of their ancestors in Cardiganshire and the children of the Welsh of Dagenham and Slough returning to the valleys of the coalfield.' Another sector of the population to arrive were wealthy exiles, especially old ladies, who decamped to hotels on the Welsh coast and in Welsh rural areas. It is estimated that Wales received at least 200,000 immigrants between 1939 and 1941 and that by 1941 the population had almost returned to the 1921 figure. The exodus of the Depression years had been reversed. It is believed that unofficial evacuation was greater than that from the official schemes.

During the war there were to be a series of evacuation schemes. The first evacuation programme was perceived as a failure and this had an impact upon the uptake of participants in subsequent schemes that took place in far more desperate circumstances. The first evacuation programme took place between 1–3 September 1939 and was an instant response to the declaration of war. 1,473,000 children, teachers and mothers were moved in a three-day period. It was a remarkable achievement, especially given that the pressure on the transport system due to the mobilisation of the armed forces. In the event this figure was one third of what had been expected. Throughout the war millions of families were to take the view that they would prefer to stay together regardless of the terrors of night-time bombardment and relentless daily air attacks.

All the evacuees were from England; there were no plans for any evacuation from Wales. This led to some criticism in Welsh Nationalist circles. Wales was being treated as an 'English reception area' and concerns were expressed for the protection of the Welsh language.

The initial arrangements for the evacuation went well. Evacuees arrived at a large number of assembly points from where they were taken to railway stations to embark on the main part of their journey. It was at this stage that problems began to emerge. In order to carry as much clothing as possible the children were over-dressed, wearing overcoats in late summer. They were not prepared for a long journey in terms of food and drink and stops had to be made to feed them. Some journeys lasted up to eight hours. On the journey from Liverpool to Pwllheli the evacuees travelled on a train without corridors and were therefore confined to a carriage for the whole journey. The major problem, however, was the lack of lavatories, which ultimately meant that by the time they arrived at their destination many evacuees had soiled themselves.

Once evacuees arrived at their destination there had been little planning in relation to their distribution. In the case of Pwllheli there was no opportunity for planning. The local authority was not scheduled for receiving any evacuees; however, it was informed on 2 September that the area was to expect 890 mothers and pre-school children from Liverpool. In the event 492 arrived.

Throughout the period September 1939 to January 1940 there was a steady trickle home. Ninety per cent of mothers evacuated with small children had returned by December 1939. The mothers were often more problematic than the children themselves and relationships with the receiving family were often strained. By January over 60 per cent of the children had returned. Of course, in these months there was no enemy action against Britain itself.

The evacuation scheme opened up a number of scars within British society. Many of the evacuee families came from the poorest of urban families; they were the 'have-nots' who did not have the means to organise a private evacuation. North Walians were shocked at the state of the clothing of children from Merseyside. Welsh local authorities spoke of 'children in rags', 'wearing garments so filthy they had to be burned' and 'some small children who were stitched into their winter apparel of calico or brown paper'. Liverpool earned the nickname of 'plimsoll city' after the footwear of many of the children. The children often came from very different backgrounds with completely different codes of behaviour. A couple from Blaenavon in Monmouthshire were surprised one evening, when going out for a walk, to be asked by their young charges whether they were going out to get drunk.

In the receiving areas, too, there was often the sense that it was the working class families who were expected to bear the brunt of the sacrifice needed to make the scheme work. There is no doubt that the evacuees were for the most part received with humanity and compassion but there was some disgruntlement in some communities that large houses with empty rooms were overlooked for evacuee accommodation.

There were certainly many mismatches in the allocation of evacuees to families. The greatest was the billeting of Roman Catholics from Liverpool in the homes of strict non-conformists in North Wales. A priest from Liverpool is said to have called for the return of children, considering that the danger to their souls was of greater import than that to their physical well-being if they were to remain in the city.

Whilst there are stories about the hardship faced by evacuees – living in homes where they received little sympathy or where they were forced to live according to a new set of rules – there are also uplifting examples. Jimmy Richie, a farmer at Ysbyty Ifan has given his story to the National Museum. At the age of nine he was evacuated with his brother from Birkenhead to Dyffryn Ardudwy in Merionethshire in September 1939. They lived on a farm. They went to Sunday school and learned Welsh from the study of Bible verses, which they then practised by talking to the local people and eventually mastered the language. Jimmy stayed on the farm throughout the war and at the end decided to stay. Evacuation completely changed the course of his life.

There are some stories about the insensitivity of receiving families to the beliefs and backgrounds of evacuees. Stories of Jewish children being forced to eat pork are common. The story of Malcolm, a Jew from London, gives a different picture and demonstrates the sensitivity of the family with whom he was billeted. Malcolm travelled to South Wales, aged five. He spent his first night sleeping on the floor of a church hall in Cardiff. Next morning he was taken in an open-topped truck to Tonypandy, seeing green hillsides for the first time in his life. He was billeted with a couple that attended a Baptist chapel every Sunday. They wrote to Malcolm's mother and asked whether he could go with them. This was agreed, but Malcolm also attended a small synagogue two evenings a week to learn Hebrew.

In May 1940 as Hitler's troops began to move through Western Europe, the government introduced a new evacuation scheme. It is a reflection on the initial scheme that only one in five eligible children were registered for evacuation at this time, when the threat of invasion was more imminent, and only one in fifty volunteered to take in evacuees. In the next three months, across Britain 213,000 children were moved and 328,000 made their own arrangements to move. The main areas that it was anticipated were most at risk of invasion were the east coast of England and London. Many London children had been evacuated to parts of Kent and Sussex in the first evacuation. For them, therefore, this was to be their second evacuation.

Don Powell, the author of *Pontypridd at War, 1939–1945*, illustrates two important features of this second evacuation scheme. Firstly, his evidence supports the fact that for many this was their second evacuation:

> Five hundred pupils from schools in Kent spilled out of the carriages and descended on the community. The train arriving at 4.05 p.m. brought 236 children and 21 helpers and teachers from schools that previously had been evacuated to Canterbury from Rochester and other Medway towns; and the train at 5.30 p.m. brought 274 children from schools previously evacuated to Faversham from Chatham, Gillingham, Rochester and Erith.

The second important point is how well prepared the town was to receive this new intake of population. The reception of the children was much improved on that of the first evacuation. The trains full of evacuees were met by crowds of cheering residents who packed the station yard accompanied by the band of the Salvation Army. The children were given a hot meal by the Education Committee and two presents – a tin of condensed milk and a tin of corned beef. After medical examinations a fleet of buses and motorcars took them to reception centres in the town and surrounding villages to meet their new 'foster parents'. This second scheme brought far more evacuees into South Wales and in particular to the coalfield valleys. Don Powell notes that in addition to the

500 evacuees that arrived at Pontypridd on the 19 May 1940, another 1,200 passed through the station on the way to the Rhondda valleys.

In May 1940 there was a dramatic turn of events on the war front as Hitler conquered Belgium, Holland and Luxembourg and French and British troops retreated to the coast at Dunkirk. France was close to capitulation and on 22 June signed an armistice with Hitler. Three days earlier, just before midnight on 19 June the air raid alert sirens sounded for the first time in Cardiff, responding to a German Luftwaffe spying mission. Wales could no longer be designated as an area 'safe' from air attack. With the conquest of northern France including the Channel ports, Normandy and Brittany, the South Wales coast was within two hours flying time of enemy aircraft.

From September 1940 the evacuation programme entered its third phase following the beginning of the Blitz, the Nazi plan to destroy the centres of the large cities in Britain and undermine the morale of the British people. There was no big evacuation event as in September 1939 and May 1940, but there was to be a constant trickle of evacuation to meet need as it arose. The purpose of evacuation was changed. No longer was it just about transferring children to a place of safety, it was also about receiving the casualties of war. This can best be illustrated by the evacuation of children and teachers into the Cardiff Rural Council area on 26 November 1940 following the bombing of Birmingham; 606 children arrived. Many had lost their homes and possessions and needed to be clothed with suitable attire for the winter months; 107 of these children required hospitalisation.

The situation in the Cardiff region was extraordinary. The Cardiff City Council area had been declared a neutral zone for evacuation purposes, that is, an area that neither received nor sent out evacuees. This was despite the fact that Cardiff had been under attack by the Luftwaffe since July. In his book *A City at War*, Dennis Morgan states that 'up until the early autumn [1940] South Wales had been visited by enemy aircraft on more occasions than anywhere else in Britain.' As early as 1 July, after seven successive nights of air raids, the City Council Education Committee asked for children to be evacuated from the city. However, it was not until after the dreadful night of death and destruction on 2 January 1941 that plans were put into place to evacuate city children to the safety of the hinterland. Throughout this whole period the Cardiff Rural Council area, including Whitchurch, only three miles from the city centre, was receiving evacuees from Birmingham despite requests that children no longer be billeted there.

In the early months of the air attacks there were no plans to evacuate children from Cardiff, however, some Cardiff families responded to an evacuation scheme, introduced in June 1940, for sending children overseas following offers of support from the US and the Dominions. 1,630 applications for evacuation abroad were received from Cardiff parents and 41 were accepted. Eleven of these children were eventually evacuated whilst another twelve who had been sailing on the *City of Benares* from Liverpool to Canada returned after a German U-Boat torpedoed the ship. Tragically, five Cardiff children were amongst the seventy-three who died in the attack, which took place on the 23 September 1940. The disaster brought a swift end to the scheme.

The bombing raid of the night of 2/3 January 1941 finally brought a change of policy in Cardiff and plans were drawn up to evacuate children from the city. Many families made their own plans, with villages on the outskirts of Cardiff receiving an influx. Children who were homeless after the raid were sent to the School Holiday Camp in Porthcawl. At the same time evacuees were still being sent from Birmingham into the Cardiff rural area. Twenty arrived at Llanederyn on 17 January. On 20 January, at the same time as pupils from Canton High School were being evacuated to the Rhondda Valley, a mile away a school in Whitchurch was receiving forty-three children from Gillingham.

On 21 January 1941 meetings were held across the city to discuss an evacuation scheme. The outcome was that out of a school population of 32,530 pupils the parents of only twenty-six per cent wished to see their children evacuated. This illustrates a great deal about the mentality of many families at this time and their desire to stick together whatever the danger and hardship.

The official evacuation scheme operated throughout April and May 1941. 4,256 Cardiff children – 13 per cent of the school population – were evacuated to the Rhondda Valley, Aberdare, Mountain Ash, Caerphilly and towns and villages in the Rhymney Valley. Further west, children from Swansea, which had been savagely attacked by the Nazi airmen, were evacuated to Carmarthenshire. Teachers volunteered to accompany the children to the evacuation areas but few actually volunteered to stay and teach. The junior members of staff were often the ones chosen to go.

The children were not entirely safe once they were evacuated. There were isolated attacks on the coalfield valleys. On 31 May 1941 German bombers hit the village of Cwmbach, near Aberdare, where thirty-nine Cardiff schoolchildren were billeted. A month earlier on 29 April four evacuee children from London died as the result of a raid on the village of Cwmparc, in the Rhondda Valley.

By the end of August 1941 55 per cent of the Cardiff evacuees had returned to the city after less than three months away. Although the Education Committee continued to encourage evacuation, the gradual drift of children back to the city went on. Teachers were attached to classes in the reception areas for the school year 1941–1942 but by September 1942 most pupils had returned. From May 1941 air raids on South Wales became less frequent, although the people of Cardiff and Swansea could never feel completely safe from attack. The months of July and August 1942 saw further attacks on Cardiff with fatalities, and Swansea suffered a serious attack in February 1943. Cardiff was the victim of another vicious attack in May 1943. By this time the vast majority of evacuees had returned to their homes, including those evacuees that had come into Wales from the large cities in England.

From the first three phases of the evacuation schemes September 1939, May 1940 and those that came during the period of the Blitz, small numbers of evacuees remained across Wales. Their reasons for staying were largely due to family circumstances. In some cases they had been orphaned, in others they had lost one parent and the other parent was in the armed forces or was engaged in war production. Some of these children demonstrated difficult behaviour. After a number of attempts at finding suitable billets for such children, they had been placed in hostels. In November 1941 the Welsh Board of Health set up a psychological service for the examination and treatment of difficult behaviour or problem cases amongst evacuee children billeted in the reception areas of Wales. Some of these children developed medical conditions that were probably a result of their circumstances. The most common of all was 'bed-wetting'. In September 1943 special allowances were introduced for householders caring for evacuees with this condition.

Parental neglect was one reason why some children remained in Wales. A teacher from Liverpool accompanying children in Caernarvonshire during 1939–1940 noted how few parents ever visited their children. Visiting was obviously an issue of finance but evidence from Cardiff Rural District Evacuation and Welfare committee reveals a core of parents who made no contact with their children. In April 1943 there were 183 unaccompanied evacuee children remaining in the district. Most had been there for over three years; 102 heard frequently from their parents, 38 seldom heard and 17 had no contact at all. It took six months for officials in consultation with the evacuating authorities to track down those parents of the seventeen children whom they had not contacted.

Those children who remained in reception areas were to be joined by another group of evacuees in June and the subsequent months of 1944. Hitler responded to the D-Day landings on 6 June by launching his secret weapon, the V1 or 'Doodlebug' as it came to be known. This was an unmanned rocket that flew with a distinctive droning noise. People soon learned that danger came when they ran out of fuel and the noise stopped. The 'flying bomb' hurtled to the ground. The first V1 was launched on 13 June and for a fortnight the attack went on as over 100 were launched per day. Casualties were severe and panic set in. Informal evacuation began first, followed by a planned scheme. On 14 July 577 evacuees and their escorts arrived at Cardiff Central station to be billeted by Cardiff Rural district council. Officials had a shock. They were expecting 400 unaccompanied children. Instead they received 577 mothers with children. The evacuees were taken to rest centres, mainly chapels in Whitchurch, Rhiwbina and Tongwynlais before being transferred to domestic billets.

Throughout July, August and September evacuees kept coming from London and the southeast. On 8 September Hitler launched another deadly weapon, the V2. These were even larger flying bombs, forty-five feet long and weighing fourteen tons. They caused a massive amount of damage when they fell to earth. The rate of V1 and V2 attacks began to decline towards the end of the year and the evacuees began to return to their homes. Many families made their own private arrangements. The first officially organised return in November 1944 involved children in North Wales going back to Merseyside. These were children from the first three phases of evacuation and some had been away from their homes for more than five years. Children from London and the south east seeking safety from the V1 and V2 attacks had gone to South Wales. The majority returned before Christmas 1944, although sporadic attacks took place until the end of March 1945.

Whilst the majority of evacuees returned home before the official end of the war the scheme was not officially wound up until March 1946. At the last meeting of the Cardiff Rural District Evacuation and Welfare Committee it was announced that there were seven accompanied evacuees, either with their mother or another adult, and two unaccompanied children still being billeted.

On 28 September 1945 a group of Belgian children returned home from Cardiff. They had been there since they had fled the Nazi invasion of their homeland in May 1940. They had been kept together and taught in their own special school.

## Works of Art

Wales was not only perceived as a potential place of safety for people, it was also identified as a suitable location for storing valuable works of art. During the First World War the National Library of Wales at Aberystwyth had provided storage for valuable books and documents from the British Museum. Given the prospect in the 1930s that a future war would be dominated by aerial bombardment, particularly of London and the south east of England, its location on the western coast of Britain was doubly attractive to those planning the preservation of Britain's art treasures if hostilities were to break out.

As early as 1933 the Ministry of Works began to plan for the evacuation of art treasures from a range of museums and galleries by establishing the Museum and Galleries Air Raid Precautions Committee. Its first task was to draw up a list of country houses suitable for the storage of works of art. These needed to be sited away from potential military objectives that would be the target of enemy bombers, for example aerodromes, munitions factories and ammunition storage dumps. North-west Wales was an ideal location.

North Wales was the chosen area for the dispersal of paintings from the National Gallery. The main sites were to be the National Library of Wales at Aberystwyth, Pritchard Jones Hall at the University of Wales, Bangor and the home of Lord Penrhyn, Penrhyn Castle in Caernarvonshire. In October 1938, as international tensions heightened over Hitler's ambitions in Czechoslovakia, 300 pictures from the National Gallery were despatched to Aberystwyth and Bangor. They were returned within a few weeks.

The National Library of Wales had within its grounds the only underground protection for art treasures completed before the outbreak of the war. It had been funded by a grant from the Treasury that had been allocated with great reluctance and on the understanding that it was a general storage facility for items from all national museums and galleries not just those housed at the National Library of Wales. It was, however, a relatively small facility.

On 23 August 1939 as the outbreak of war was seemingly inevitable, Sir Kenneth Clark sought permission to begin the evacuation of pictures from the National Gallery to locations expected to be safe havens. Between 25 August and 6 of September over 1,000 paintings and other boxes of artefacts and documents were transported to Aberystwyth and Bangor. It was an operation that would have been a credit to any of the military services. On the night of Saturday 2 September, just hours before Neville Chamberlain made his declaration of war, six special freight trains made their way from Camden Goods Yard in North London to Bangor on the North Wales coast. Armed police and soldiers stood guard at every tunnel, bridge and level crossing along the route. The 218 paintings on board constituted the most valuable cargo ever carried on a British railway train.

The concept of Wales as a safe haven was undermined when France capitulated to Hitler in June 1940 and Nazi forces took up positions along the north-west coast of France. Wales fell into range of the enemy bombers. Many of the paintings housed at the National Library occupied the top floor.

At Pritchard Jones Hall, Bangor and Penrhyn Castle other issues had emerged. The heating system at Pritchard Jones Hall worked erratically and it was not proving possible to provide the necessary consistent storage conditions for the paintings held there. However, it was matters of security that concerned Martin Davies, the Assistant Keeper responsible for the paintings. In February 1940 the University of Wales student magazine, *Omnibus*, carried an article about there being National Gallery pictures stored in Pritchard Jones Hall. There was some discussion about invoking the Defence of the Realm Act to prevent further disclosures. Martin Davies arrived at some startling conclusions about the loyalty of the local population. Firstly, he questioned the loyalty of some of the British Legion members who had been recruited to provide security at Pritchard Jones Hall. Presumably they could have been the source of information to the student magazine. More seriously he wrote to his superiors that he was

… feeling considerably agitated about the safety of the pictures … not so much on account of danger from bombing as from civil disturbance on a large scale … Pritchard Jones Hall and Penrhyn cannot be effectively defended against the mob.

Francis Rawlings, scientific adviser at the National Gallery who worked closely with Martin Davies wrote in a similar vein to the Office of Works:

Our concern is … with the possibility of activities by the 5th column. You will recall that I mentioned to you in a conversation my own gleanings of local information about this.

N.J. McCamley, author of the book *Saving Britain's Art Treasures*, states that the RAF, which had commissioned an underground bomb store at Llanberis, shared these fears. He quotes the depot's logbook as stating that

There is a shortage of civilian staff, who are all local, Welsh, and very nationalistic – more interested in Home Rule than work. Likewise the Security Wardens are Welsh and are not considered trustworthy.

These are quite extraordinary claims. It will be seen that there was a great deal of support for many of the ideas of the Welsh Nationalist Party in the Caernarvonshire area, especially in relation to the status of the Welsh language; however, there was limited support for the anti-war stance taken by the party and the numbers seeking to become conscientious objectors were few. It was a major leap to identify support for nationalist ideas with a willingness to take part in civilian disturbances and riots to back Nazi invasion attempts. Nevertheless these views of Davies and Rawlins were important in informing their belief that alternative accommodation should be found for the paintings.

An intriguing situation had also developed at Penrhyn Castle. There appears to have been a breakdown in the relationship between Martin Davies and Lord Penrhyn, the former complaining to his superiors about the obstructive attitude of the latter. He complained that he was celebrating the war 'by being fairly constantly drunk' and that pictures were in danger from his stumbling around the dining room with his dog. On 5 June 1940 he reported that this particular danger had been removed because Lord Penrhyn had smashed up his car and, 'himself a little'.

In September 1940 Lord Penrhyn made retrospective demands for rent. Davies was shocked that the country house owners seemed mainly to be interested in making money and did not appreciate that by having the paintings stored at their properties they had avoided the inconvenience of having evacuees or the military compulsorily placed in their houses. He wrote to the Office of Works that 'their willingness to make sacrifice in war does not seem to be great, and one cannot help suspecting that of such are the followers of Petain made.' Davies was not slow in coming forward with his concerns for the paintings or with his rather idiosyncratic political analysis. He was clearly frustrated by local attitudes and particularly that of Lord Penrhyn at a time when Britain was facing the serious danger of an enemy invasion. However, given the antipathy that Welsh speaking, nationalist-minded working people of the area would have had for the anglicised landed estate owners, his proposition that both would be ready and willing to support an invasion force is barely credible.

Francis Rawlins had long held the view that the paintings should be kept at an underground depository and in July 1940 he was authorised to find underground storage for them. In the meantime there was a further dispersal of the paintings from Pritchard Jones Hall and Penrhyn Castle to the Eagle Tower at Caernarvon Castle, Plas-yr-Bryn in Bontnewydd and Crosswood House, near Aberystwyth.

Rawlins began his search for a suitable underground storage and after investigating and rejecting a number of sites, on 17 September 1940 he discovered Manod Quarry above the village of Blaenau Ffestiniog and declared it to be suitable. It was sited at the end of a five-mile track in Snowdonia, in a remote and desolate location 1,750 feet above sea level. It was a disused slate quarry, which consisted of a series of worked-out chambers, some of which were over 100 feet high.

Justification for protecting the paintings came on 12 October 1940 when the National Gallery in Trafalgar Square was hit by a bomb that exploded and destroyed one of the rooms used for display. Another seven bombs hit the building during the next month and a further bomb fell on 17 April 1941. At the time of these raids Francis Rawlins was busy supervising an even safer haven for the paintings. Five of the vast chambers were adapted so that they could provide the conditions in which the art treasures would be preserved. Each chamber had its own air-conditioning system which ensured four changes of air an hour, and a constant atmosphere of 65F and 42 per cent humidity. 5,000 tons of slate was removed from the mountain entrance to create access for the lorries with their valuable assets.

It took until August 1941 to complete the conversion process. Between 12 August and 16 September, 2,000 pictures including masterpieces by the likes of Gainsborough, Hogarth, Constable, Turner, Monet, Degas and Rembrandt were transferred to Manod in lorries provided by the GWR and LMS railway companies. There were few problems, except for the large painting by Van Dyck of 'Charles I on Horseback'. The canvas was 3.7 metres high and weighed half a ton. A road under one of the bridges on its journey from Penrhyn had to be lowered to enable it to reach its destination.

Once the existence of Manod became known the trustees of the National Gallery received requests from other institutions and private collectors asking for storage space at the quarry. By the end of the war over thirty collections were represented there, including paintings from Buckingham Palace, Windsor Castle and Hampton Court.

Life in the quarry, once the pictures were established there, reverted to the routine that constituted the day-to-day activity of the National Gallery before the war. Works were restored and the pictures were catalogued. Sir Martin Davies, who with his colleague, Francis Rawlins had played an essential role in protecting the paintings in the early years of the war, produced a series of catalogues that became renowned for their new approach to the study of pictures.

The detail of the story of the National Gallery paintings has become known since the 1980s and is described in depth by N.J. McCamley. It is an aspect of wartime history that raises certain philosophical questions. The cost of converting Manod was approximately £17,000, the equivalent of nearly £700,000 today. How important in the whole scope of the war was this project? Was it necessary to preserve these paintings at a time when human beings were being slaughtered in their thousands each day? How would the miners of North and South Wales, contemporaries of Martin Davies, also working in the bowels of the earth have viewed this episode in the context of the conditions in which they worked and lived?

Whatever one's view on these questions, this project represents a remarkable episode in the story of wartime Wales. Together with the location of munitions factories, air force training, soldiers' training, and the provision of homes for evacuees, it indicates how the authorities perceived the importance of the strategic position of Wales to the British war effort. Even following the Fall of France which brought Wales into the range of enemy bombers, it was viewed as being a less vulnerable part of Britain. With the exception of the Bristol Channel ports, Pembroke Dock and Milford Haven, this was largely true.

# Chapter Two

# Attitudes to the War – Pacifists, Nationalists and Communists

The Second World War has been described as 'the least unexpected war in history'. When Prime Minister Neville Chamberlain made his historic radio broadcast on Sunday 3 September 1939 there was little surprise at his declaration that the country was at war. There was also a huge measure of support.

When war had been declared twenty-five years previously in 1914 there had been outpourings of jingoistic support verging on hysteria. This was not the case in 1939. A spokesperson for Swansea Council talked of 'relief in many quarters that the war of nerves was over and the decision had been made'. Ever since Hitler's invasion of Czechoslovakia in March 1939, the introduction of conscription and an increased level of civil defence activity, there had been an expectation that hostilities would be inevitable.

In the Gwent mining town of Abertillery it was announced that the news had been received with 'calmness and resignation'. Resignation was an appropriate choice of word; this was a war that no-one wanted. Influential in communities across Wales was a generation of men and women who had the first-hand experience of what it meant to be 'at war'. Many had fought and knew about the privations, brutality and psychological damage of warfare. Others had witnessed the stringencies of life on the Home Front and the loss of friends, relatives, sons and fathers. Throughout the 1930s there had been a prevailing sense that another war should be avoided at all costs.

In 1938 following the Munich Agreement with Hitler that seemed to offer hope that war might be averted, Neville Chamberlain told Conservative Party members: 'When I think of those four terrible years [of the First World War], and I think of the seven million young men who were killed, the thirteen million who were maimed and mutilated, I felt it was my duty to strain every nerve to avoid a repetition.' His words would resonate throughout most villages, towns and cities.

On the other hand there was an increasing awareness that the Nazi regime in Germany was ruthlessly determined to pursue its ambitions regardless of international diplomacy and opinion elsewhere. The invasion of Czechoslovakia in March 1939 and that of Poland at the end of August led to an increasing acceptance that military aggression required a military response, despite inner fears of the terrible outcome that would ensue.

To describe the response to the outbreak of war as being one of support is, however, a generalisation that requires some qualification. The 1930s had witnessed deep social division and disagreement about domestic policy. Division was equally as marked in response to foreign affairs. There were individuals and organisations that had been severely critical of government foreign policy from a range of different perspectives. There was not, therefore, total agreement that the declaration of war should be supported. Welsh Nationalists, Communists and pacifists were small in number but vocal critics of government policy. Their influence varied in different areas of Wales.

There were more conscientious objectors in Wales than in any other part of Great Britain. By July 1940 2.56 per cent of men called-up in Wales were registered as conscientious objectors, compared with 1.3 per cent in England and 1.46 per cent in Scotland. Compared with the First World War the figures were low, although it was claimed in one national newspaper that the level of opposition to the war in Wales was used in Nazi propaganda. Such statements appear to have had an impact, for when it was decided to relocate art treasures from country houses to a central underground depository; fear of a Welsh Nationalist uprising was cited as one of the reasons.

Such views are hard to reconcile with a realistic assessment of the support for anti-war nationalist opinion at the start of the war and the attitudes of members of the Welsh Nationalist Party. MI5's list of suspects in Wales – published in 2002 and reproduced in *Hitler's Celtic Echo* by Ivor Wynne Jones – identified 156 potential traitors during the war, including six members only of the WNP. The vast majority were either members of the British Union of Fascists or were foreign nationals, mainly Germans and Italians.

Details of the WNP at this time mostly come from D. Hywel Davies's book *The Welsh Nationalist Party, 1925–1945*. The WNP had a paid up membership of between 2,000 and 3,000 in 1939. There were 7,000 monthly subscribers to their newspaper *Y Ddraig Goch*. For many of these people this represented an expression of interest rather than a direct commitment. Formed in 1925, the Welsh Nationalist Party made little impact outside Wales, and within Wales it was primarily limited to members of the intelligentsia. Its membership consisted largely of teachers, lecturers and non-conformist ministers. Its favoured meeting place was the chapel vestry rather than the workingmen's club. Support was concentrated in north-west Wales, especially Caernarvonshire.

The Party came to popular attention in 1936 when three prominent members committed arson by burning down huts built to house construction workers, at the site of a planned Air Ministry bombing school where the RAF could practice specialist bombing techniques, as detailed in the previous chapter. The bombing school site was at Penyberth on the Lleyn Peninsula. It had originally been planned for Abbotsbury in Dorset but public support had prevented this happening due to the threat posed to an ancient swannery. For those concerned with the preservation of the Welsh language, religious heritage and the environment there was an equally sound case for not locating the bombing school at Penyberth. At the 1935 Welsh Nationalist Party conference the Baptist minister Reverend Lewis Valentine informed his audience that he was urging fellow Baptists to adopt Gandhian tactics of civil disobedience to prevent an invasion of militarism into the area, and urged party members to follow suit.

On 8 September 1936 Reverend Valentine, WNP President Saunders Lewis and the poet D.J. Williams burned down the huts and then handed themselves over to the police. They appeared at Caernarvon Assizes in October 1936 supported by large crowds outside the courtroom. The judge ordered a re-trial. This took place in England. All three of the accused refused to accept the authority of the court and refused to speak in English. They were sentenced to nine months imprisonment. Their response to the legal processes in a sense moved their protest into a different arena, that is, the status of the Welsh language.

Large meetings followed their release, including one attended by 12,000 people in Caernarvon. It would seem that the widespread sympathetic support for Valentine, Williams and Lewis influenced later interpretations of attitudes in this part of Wales, including German intelligence.

By 1938 Saunders Lewis, who had lost his job as a lecturer at Swansea University, recognised that the party had failed to build on the popular response following the arson attack in terms of recruits. He believed that there had been a lost opportunity and it is ironic that the early years of the war saw a mushrooming of airfields and military training not only in north-west Wales but across the country as a whole.

The Penyberth protest was of great significance because it highlighted the lack of legal status of the Welsh language and radicalised a number of writers such as Dr Gwenallt Jones and Waldo Williams. An agenda related to the preservation of Welsh culture and the specific individuality of Wales within the United Kingdom was more strongly generated and it led to a more positive response from other political parties.

As the outbreak of war approached the WNP gained a wider prominence again. At the party's 1938 conference the policy of Wales' neutrality in the case of war was declared:

> The Nationalist Party will not take part in England's wars. Therefore no Welsh Nationalist may join in this war nor agree to work in armament factories or help the war in any way.

Saunders Lewis argued that the main cause of modern war was imperialism and that the threat of war in 1938 was a result of a clash between rival imperialist powers. Whilst Hitler may have broken his word and oppressed smaller nations, it should be remembered that England had not kept its promises to the Arabs, the Jews or to India. The war was not a Welsh war. The views of Saunders Lewis expressed in *Y Ddraig Goch* were interpreted by some as being sympathetic to a fascist point of view and it does appear that Nazi intelligence was of the opinion that there was the potential to develop an embryonic group of supporters in areas of north-west Wales. They attempted to establish a Welsh National radio service in July 1940 using a guardsman from Treallaw, William Humphreys Griffiths, a prisoner of war, as their spokesperson. Although some recordings were made, none were ever broadcast. Further evidence of the attitude of Nazi intelligence comes from the memoirs of Sydney Pritchard which were published in 2007. Sydney was amongst the Welsh Guards that were taken prisoner in France in 1940. Eventually he found himself in a prisoner of war camp in Poland. One day he was taken for interview by high ranking German officers:

> I was ordered to answer the following questions. Was I a Welshman? Did my family live in Wales? Where in Wales did they live? Why was I in the British army (being a Welshman)? And why did I fight for England, being a Welshman? ... For comfort, good living quarters and a limited amount of freedom, they wanted my cooperation, to wear a German uniform and join their ranks. They also wanted me to do radio broadcasting and non combat fighting. Without any hesitation on my part, my reply was a firm NO!

There was some unease within the Welsh Nationalist Party with the position taken towards the war and some members complained that the party gave the impression that it was more of an anti-war movement than a movement for Welsh Home Rule. One prominent member, Ambrose Bebb, chose to resign. Many quietly chose to join the armed forces and dropped out of party political activity. One member said, 'there is something more important than keeping Blaid alive. I do not believe in putting anything in the way of licking Hitler.' Hostility to members persuaded many to keep a low profile. A public meeting in Pembroke in November 1940 had to be terminated due to opposition.

Within the party there was a strong pacifist element. This meant that there was a complex mixture of motives for party members' individual responses to the war. The party agreed to oppose the introduction of conscription and 'cunning' militarist plans such as ARP wardens. Members should not accept being forced into the army of a foreign country, especially one which was guilty of neglecting Welsh interests.

It was clear following the first days of military registration in June 1939 that there was to be no massive protest campaign. There was further disappointment for the WNP leaders. Many party members who opposed military registration quoted their religious and moral opposition to war ahead of their nationalist objections. In November 1939, for example, of six WNP members who pleaded Welsh Nationalism at the

Caernarvon tribunal none made it their sole grounds, but mentioned it in reinforcing a pacifist objection.

The great significance of quoting exclusively nationalist objections was that the tribunals did not accept nationalism as being a matter of conscience whereas to express objection in a Christian context was recognised as valid grounds for exemption from military service. Imprisonment awaited those who insisted on stating a purely nationalist point of view.

The first person to choose an uncompromising nationalist attitude is an interesting example. John G. Brooks was a Cornishman, known as John Legonna, living in Oxfordshire. His Celtic origins had encouraged him to join the WNP. He argued that as a Celt and a Welsh Nationalist, he did not believe that the English and Anglo-Saxons had any right to conscript the Celtic people into their armies. He was not a pacifist and would be prepared to fight if the Celtic people could make decisions for themselves. He was placed on the military register and became the first of the twelve nationalists to be imprisoned for their objections during the war.

In January 1940, Gwyn Jones of Coedpoeth, near Wrexham and Dafydd Williams of Caernarvon joined John Legonna on the register and became the first nationalists in Wales to be jailed for continuing to resist military service. Amongst the twelve who were imprisoned was A.O.H. Jarman, the editor of *Y Ddraig Goch*.

Given the commitment of the vast majority of the British people to the defeat of Nazi Germany, those nationalists who stood by their principles ran the gauntlet of public hostility. Many lost their jobs, especially if they worked for local government. The most prominent amongst them was Iorwerth Peate from the Folk Studies Department of the National Museum.

It is hard to understand the fears expressed in some quarters of the possibility of a Welsh Nationalist uprising on the basis of a relatively small protest by a few committed individuals, although it is now known that the German High Command had sought 'fifth column' assistance from Welsh Nationalists. They appear to have been deluded in this respect due to the opinions of one or two individuals who were collaborating with them. These may have included William Joyce, 'Lord Haw-Haw' who had spent some time in Wales and Arthur George Owen a double agent who worked for the *Abwehr*, German Counter Intelligence and MI5.

As the realities of war became more evident by the middle of 1940, the party went into relative hibernation and did not make a significant reappearance on to the national scene until 1943 when the party decided to contest a by-election with an agenda focusing primarily on the need to preserve the Welsh culture and language.

Prominent party member and President of the party from 1945, Gwynfor Evans was a leading protagonist against the war as a Christian pacifist and secretary of the Peace Pledge Union. Pacifism had grown in strength in the years following the First World War in both religious and political circles. In the late 1930s the movement faced the dilemma created by the brutal successes of the aggressive military actions of totalitarian regimes – the Japanese in Manchuria, the Italians in Abyssinia, the success of Franco in Spain and Hitler's expansionism in central Europe – and many individuals became uncomfortable with their views. At the start of the war there were a small number of MPs who were pacifists, whilst the umbrella organisation for opponents of physical violence, the Peace Pledge Union, claimed to have over 100,000 members in Britain.

The Peace Pledge Union actively campaigned on the issue of conscientious objection. It bought large houses in Cardiff, Penarth and Carmarthen. Here, they organised mock-tribunals to provide guidance upon how to act at the actual tribunals in order to become a registered conscientious objector.

At one session of the South Wales Conscientious Objectors Tribunal at Carmarthen, twenty-five applicants came from the small villages of Crwbin and Llangerdeine in the Gwendraeth Valley, fourteen of whom were employed as miners at the Pentremawr Colliery, Pontyberem. The presiding judge had no doubt that there had been a 'mass production of conscience'. He claimed that 'There is no other district in the kingdom where there is such a large proportion of conscientious objectors.' He visited the area the following day and discovered that 'young men who had seldom visited a place of worship had suddenly become regular attendants at prayer and chapel meetings.'

There is no doubt, however, that nearly all conscientious objectors were people of sincere and devoutly-held views. The non-conformist movement had long been influential in promoting pacifism, and ministers such as George Maitland Llewellyn Davies were prominent in advocating such a stance. Pacifists found it more difficult to maintain their position once the 'phoney war' was over and the traumatic events surrounding the Fall of France and the Blitz brought the fierce realities of war to the 'back-door'. The Presbyterian Church of Wales, for example, modified its attitude and called off its campaign to call upon the government to convene a conference of all nations for the settlement of international differences. The Welsh Congregationalists, however, held firm to their convictions and called for an immediate armistice and peace negotiations at their annual conferences in 1941 and 1942. The Llanelli Council for Evangelical Churches called upon the government to declare its peace aims in July 1941.

Those who appeared before the conscientious objectors tribunals and were accepted as having moral, humanitarian or religious grounds for objection were usually registered as COs. They were either ordered to take up approved work, usually in agriculture or to continue in the work that they were undertaking. Some were registered for non-combatant duties in the armed forces. Public opinion varied towards the objectors. There was a certain pride in the fact that tolerance of pacifist views could be sustained. Pacifists who undertook social work on behalf of a Quaker Settlement in the Rhondda found the people 'remarkably tolerant', having expected hostility. On the other hand some found that work colleagues were bitter towards them and some refused to speak to them. One has written about his anguish that his mother was victimised and spat at in the street by other women.

Not all COs opposed the war on religious grounds. As well as the Welsh Nationalists previously mentioned, there were also numbers of socialists who argued against support for the war. These included some members of the Labour Party, such as S.O. Davies, the MP for Merthyr Tydfil who took an abstentionist viewpoint throughout the war years and refused to give unqualified support to events such as War Weapons Weeks in his constituency. Members of the small Independent Labour Party argued that the war was one between capitalist powers and that it was wrong to kill fellow workers in other countries.

One I.L.P. activist who became a conscientious objector was Lance Rogers, a collier from Cefn Coed, near Merthyr. Lance Rogers had given up the opportunity of a scholarship to Ruskin College at Oxford to fight on the Republican side in the Spanish Civil War. He served with the British Battalion of the International Brigade for twenty-one months and was wounded at the Battle of Brunete in July 1937. He was called up to serve in the British Army soon after the declaration of war, but applied for registration as a CO. The South Wales tribunal surprisingly registered him unconditionally in April 1940, but this decision was overturned by the Central Appellate Tribunal for Conscientious Objectors in London. His name was removed from the register of COs. This meant that he was no longer exempt from military service. He was duly called up to serve in the South Wales Borderers. On his refusal to do so he was court-martialled and sentenced to ninety-three days imprisonment.

There were also conscientious objectors who were supporters of fascism. The recently released MI5 Welsh Suspect List includes John Hooper Harvey who was an evacuated civil servant living in Prestatyn who worked for the ancient monuments branch of the Ministry of Works. He was a member of the Imperial Fascist League and registered as a CO on political and ethical grounds. The Suspect List also included a woman from Ystrad Rhondda who appeared before a tribunal in Cardiff following her refusal to serve in the Women's Land Army. At her hearing she expressed her support for Nazism.

In the first two years of the war all those who appeared before conscientious objector tribunals were male. The introduction of conscription for women in December 1941 made it illegal for any woman to refuse to do war work or enter the armed services. Young women began to appear before tribunals during 1942. Most were dealt with sympathetically and were registered for social, hospital or land work. Some objected to any kind of war work. These included a number of Jehovah's Witnesses, several of whom served short prison sentences. One, Iris Cooze, was interviewed by Leigh Verrill-Rhys and Deidre Beddoe for their collection of writings by Welsh women on the Second World War, *Parachutes and Petticoats*. Iris was a Jehovah's Witness working full-time as a 'pioneer' in Abercarn, Monmouthshire. She refused to take up war work. On her seventh appearance in court she was sent to Cardiff Prison. A young and innocent girl, she found herself working alongside prostitutes.

Other opponents of the war, in addition to conscientious objectors, found themselves in gaol during the war. Three young nationalists spent Christmas of 1941 in prison after they had walked away from the singing of 'God Save the King' at the end of a summer concert show on Aberystwyth promenade. This was probably a result of the attentions of the chief inspector of police in Aberystwyth who was particularly vigilant in his attentions to anti-war activists. The most famous case involving him concerned the father and son T.E. and Islwyn Nicholas. They were gaoled in Swansea and Brixton between July and October 1940.

T.E. Nicholas was a minister, dentist, bard, a protagonist for the Welsh language and a communist. He had been the minister at Capel Sion in the small village of Glais in the lower Swansea Valley. Here he gained a reputation for holding revolutionary views and speaking up for the disadvantaged. In 1914 he moved to Cardiganshire where he became active in organising trades unionism amongst farm labourers. Throughout the First World War he promoted pacifism across South Wales. In 1920 he joined the embryonic Communist Party of Great Britain and in the 1930s opposed fascist aggression and criticised the British government's policy of appeasement. Nevertheless he followed the CPGB when it declared the war between Britain and Germany as a capitalist war which was not in the interests of the international working class.

Professor David Howell, in a short pamphlet about T.E. Nicholas states that he 'fell victim to a witch-hunt'. He was exposed to the vengeful spite of the chief constable who was determined to put him behind bars for his pro-Russian sympathies. Nicholas and his son were charged with 'acts prejudicial to the public safety and the defence of the realm'. They were also accused of endeavouring to impede recruitment into the armed forces. The evidence against the two men was the presence in their house of a war map, published by the *Daily Express*, with German flags pinned on it to show the course of the war. They were in Brixton Prison at the time of the Blitz along with Fascist supporters who cheered as the bombs fell. T.E. Nicholas penned 150 sonnets on toilet paper during this period. The two men were eventually released following a campaign in which the South Wales Miners Federation (SWMF) was very much involved. Within the SWMF the Communist Party was an effective pressure group.

The Communist Party were a small organisation, but had significant influence within certain trades unions. The SWMF was the largest union in Wales with over 120,000 members. The president, Arthur Horner, was a CPGB member, as were several other members of the union executive. Throughout the 1930s SWMF policy relating to foreign affairs followed that of the far left of the Labour Party and the CPGB. It was highly critical of the national government on international affairs. It had been most vociferous in its opposition to non-intervention in Spain, but also to the government's policy on the Italian invasion of Abyssinia, its participation in the dismemberment of Czechoslovakia and with its repeated refusals to enter into meaningful negotiations with the Russian government.

It was to be expected that the CPGB would welcome a government decision to stand against the Nazi regime, but the ten year non-aggression pact signed by Hitler and Stalin on 24 August 1939 generated confusion. On 2 September, the day after the invasion of Poland and the day before Britain's declaration of war, the CPGB issued a pamphlet entitled *How to Win the War*. A month later the Central Committee in Moscow told the British Communist Party that it had been guilty of an error in its analysis. The war was an Imperialist war and it was the duty of Marxists to fight the British ruling class.

This *volte-face* placed many individual members of the CPGB in a difficult position, not least the president of SWMF Arthur Horner. There is much anecdotal evidence to suggest that he was in favour of the original position and had difficulty in finding the new party line tenable. However, party activists within the SWMF were soon agitating for the union to take a policy position against the war. A sufficient number of union lodges sent in anti-war resolutions to the union headquarters to force the calling of a special conference. This took place in February 1940. The conference deferred its decision to the local lodges and a debate was held up and down the South Wales coalfield that ultimately led to a three to one vote in favour of the war.

This debate took place before the war moved out of its 'phoney' period. Many regarded it as a major distraction to the job in hand and certainly many CPGB members did not pursue the party's policy with their usual conviction. To suggest that there were as many as 30,000 miners who directly opposed the war would not be realistic. However, what the vote does indicate was the ingrained support for activists who were identified in supporting working class causes in the years prior to the war.

Although defeated in their 'stop-the-war' campaign the Communist Party and some left-wing members of the Labour Party were continually critical of the government. They opposed the tactic of conscientious objection and engaged in debates on aspects of government policy that affected the people's daily lives. This is best exemplified by an examination of the policy of the South Wales Miners Federation. Arthur Horner told the organisation's annual conference in April 1940 that the change from peace to war could not lessen the obligation of a trade union to safeguard the working and living conditions of its members. War was not only terrible in the sense that blood would be shed in battles on land, sea and air, it was also horribly expensive. The burden of the expense would fall on the shoulders of the working people.

In the first eighteen months of the war the union became involved in campaigns against the rising cost of living due to the war and in related demands for increased benefits to pensioners, dependents of members of the armed forces, and the abolition of the means test. The union affiliated to the People's Vigilance Movement.

The People's Vigilance Movement was most active between May 1940 and January 1941, the very period in which Britain was facing its fiercest direct attack from Nazi bombers. Although Chamberlain had been replaced as prime minister and Labour Party leaders had joined a coalition government, the PVM campaigned for a People's Convention to take place to press for a 'People's Government' which would be truly representative of the people of Britain. At local level the idea was that 'vigilance committees' would be established to monitor price rises and profiteering.

The SWMF was the only major organisation of consequence to sign the manifesto of the PVM and was one of only four unions that sent delegates to the People's Convention when it met on 12 January 1941 in Holborn Hall in London. In all there were exactly 100 Welsh delegates out of the 2,234 that attended. Many were members of the Communist Party, such as Will Paynter, miners' agent in the Rhymney Valley, but others were members of the Labour Party. Some, like Councillor Mabel Lewis, from Mountain Ash, who chaired a conference of the PVM in South Wales, were expelled from the Labour Party for their involvement.

The support for the People's Convention was remarkable because it took place at a time when the security of Britain was being seriously threatened. It symbolised a sense that although there was a vital 'pulling together' in the face of adversity, there were strong undercurrents of discontent that sought expression. Although the government claimed that the Convention was not representative of any large body of working class opinion and gave no cause for alarm, it responded by suppressing the newspaper of the Communist Party, the *Daily Worker*, several days after the Convention met.

The Communist Party retained its oppositionist line against the government until June 1941 when the Soviet Union was invaded by Nazi Germany. Full support for the war quickly followed and 'Anglo-Russian solidarity committees' were established in communities to raise funds for the Russian government. In some workplaces it generated a renewed vigour in support of production drives. Support for the prosecution of the war was not uncritical, however. For example, it campaigned for the opening of a second front in Europe at an early date to support the Russian war effort.

Throughout the war there was a continuous trickle of conscientious objection with each successive call-up to the armed forces and in the case of women to war work, mainly on religious grounds. Of the political organisations that opposed the war only the ILP, which had three MPs, all from Scotland, had an institutional presence. In Merthyr Tydfil around the Troedyrhiw area, the ILP had three local councillors. Towards the end of the war in May 1945 an ILP candidate polled 13,722 votes in a by-election in Newport and only failed to beat the Conservative, National Government candidate by 2,500 votes. In the same month the Welsh Nationalist Party and the Trotskyite, Revolutionary Communist Party both put up by-election candidates in Neath and polled over 8,000 votes between them. The context for opposition was very different by this time, however, as war was coming to an end and the debate on post-war reconstruction dominated.

The reality was, throughout the war, that the vast majority of the population recognised the necessity of opposing the Nazi threat. Misgivings were expressed about the conduct of the war, the extent of wartime controls and in the last two years about government plans for the future in post-war Wales. That such expressions of discontent and concern were possible was in a way a justification for both fighting and supporting the war effort. They represented the democratic freedoms that were threatened by the enemy.

## Chapter Three

# The Fall of France and the Impact on Wales – Air Attack and the Return of 'The Depression'

Once war was declared on 3 September 1939 Britain was committed to sending troops to France. By the middle of October 158,000 British troops of the British Expeditionary Force (BEF), were serving in northern France and Belgium. A significant number were with Welsh regiments. The number of troops grew to 394,165 by May 1940.

After months of inactivity, action came swiftly. Hitler's war machine invaded Holland on 10 May and broke through into France on 14 May. The BEF were surrounded on three sides. On 21 May they were ordered to counter-attack near Arras. The attack could not be sustained and the order came that they were to withdraw to the Channel port of Dunkirk for evacuation.

The journey to the coast was chaotic. As well as the soldiers there were thousands of civilian refugees fleeing from the fighting. Many were on horse-drawn carts laden with their possessions. Progress was further impeded by frequent interruptions as German planes flew in low and sprayed the roads with bullets. Approximately 20,000 men died in the campaign and another 40,000 were taken prisoner. These included 100 Company of the Monmouthshire Royal Engineers who had performed valuable work delaying the enemy advance by blowing up bridges and fuel stores. Two companies of the Welsh Guards fought on for two days after their comrades had taken to the sea. Two Welshmen, Phil Phillips and Eric North, told their stories to the *South Wales Echo* in 1990. Phil was shot in the leg whilst riding a motorcycle and drove into a ditch.

When he recovered consciousness there were two Germans standing over him. He spent the next five years in a prisoner of war camp in East Prussia. Eric was wounded when hit by shrapnel from a bomb. He was treated by German surgeons and when fit enough to walk he marched through Holland and then travelled on barges across Germany to Mariesberg in Poland for 'five dreary years' in Stalag XXB. A Dutch farm worker managed to get a message home to his mother to let her know that he was alive.

Over 330,000 men were evacuated from Dunkirk. The operation to get them off the beaches took nearly nine days. In addition to naval ships there was an armada of smaller craft sailed by volunteers. Some men had to wait for days before they were able to board a boat and all the time the enemy aircraft rained down bombs. Many of the ships on the rescue mission were sunk themselves. Despite the maelstrom of activity, Claude Shore from Cardiff told the *South Wales Echo* that his abiding impression of Dunkirk was the 'sheer orderliness of it all … We had every confidence we'd get off. There was no panic.'

Amongst the ships supporting the evacuation was a paddle steamer, well known to holidaymakers in South Wales. The *Glen Gower* had spent the previous eighteen years of its existence ferrying day-trippers between Barry and Minehead. At the start of the war it had been commissioned for minesweeping in the North Sea. During the Dunkirk operation the *Glen Gower* made three journeys to the beaches. The first trip was the most dramatic. A shell burst under the ship's stern and another smashed through the deck and exploded amongst troops crammed into the stoker's quarters. Ten men died and six were wounded. Whilst this was happening men were still piling on board. 1,500 men sailed into Harwich with the flag at half-mast in honour of those who had died.

Another 'little ship' with a Welsh connection at Dunkirk was the *Marie Llewellyn* skippered by Captain David 'Potato' Jones. He was a well-known character who owned three tramp steamers and operated out of Swansea. He had become famous during the Spanish Civil War for defying Franco's blockade of Bilbao and reputedly providing guns to Republican supporters under the cover of delivering shipments of potatoes.

The story of Dunkirk was portrayed in the press as a major achievement, and in many ways it was. To rescue so many men in the face of overwhelming enemy superiority was phenomenal. However, it was a part of that chain of events that led to the capitulation of France and the signing of an armistice with Hitler on 21 June 1940. The Fall of France had significant consequences for Wales. No longer could Wales be described as a 'safe haven' from enemy attack.

The Luftflotte 3 section of the Luftwaffe established itself in the north-west regions of France, including Normandy and Brittany. The South Wales coast was within two hours flying time. The navigation of the aircraft was helped by the expert use of radio-beam systems. Radio stations were established at ports such as Cherbourg. Liverpool and Birkenhead, where the Cammel Laird shipbuilding yards were located, were at the northern limit of the range of the radio beams. This meant that it was not just South Wales that was within range of the bombers; the whole of North Wales was vulnerable too.

The speed with which the Luftwaffe took advantage of its new strategic position was both remarkable and frightening. As early as the first hours of the morning of 20 June 1940 Cardiff received its first visitation from enemy aircraft. A single aeroplane attacked the docks and dropped sixteen bombs. On 28 June bombs were dropped on RAF Sealand in Flintshire. Wales was now a theatre of war. In June 1940, the defensive squadrons of aircraft were all based in the south-east of England. Targets in Wales and the north-west of England were, therefore, undefended.

Within North Wales, airfields and the Vickers-Armstrong factory at Broughton were the main targets for attack, although it was Liverpool, Birkenhead and shipping in the Irish Sea that were the principle objectives for the enemy. To attack Merseyside the German planes either flew up the eastern part of Wales to reach their destination or, from the more western parts of France they flew up the Welsh coast, across Cardigan Bay, turned east over the Irish Sea, and continued parallel to the North Wales coast towards their targets.

South Wales was also a prime target area with the ports of Newport, Cardiff and Swansea along the coast and vital resource centres such as the coalfield and the steelworks at Ebbw Vale and Port Talbot close by. Of particular military importance were the munitions factories at Glascoed and Bridgend, the major RAF base at St Athan and other smaller airfields. Further west in Pembrokeshire there were more airfields, the deep sea port of Milford Haven and the oil refineries at Pembroke Dock.

The air war had three distinct phases. The first was from June to September 1940 and included the Battle of Britain, the second was the period of the Blitz, September 1940 through till June 1941 and the third was from June 1941 until May 1943 when attacks became more sporadic but were nevertheless still brutal.

It is difficult to determine the exact start of the Battle of Britain – the Luftwaffe campaign to destroy the RAF, its airfields and aircraft factories. In some textbooks it is 13 August 1940, 'Eagle Day', but the attack on the British mainland had been ongoing since the Fall of France. Individual bombers had visited cities and other strategic sites in an intermittent and random manner. Their intention was to give training to Luftwaffe pilots, to gather information for further raids, to cause damage to docks and other installations and to strike fear into the hearts of civilians. During that period up to 13 August Cardiff had had seventy-one air raids. The gradual wearing down of the population had begun. Many a night's sleep was broken, daytime work schedules were disrupted, time was spent in mainly damp and seat-less shelters and there was fear as sirens sounded and engines droned above.

The first casualties of the air war in Wales occurred on 9 July. A lone bomber made a daytime attack on Cardiff docks. A direct hit was made on the sailing ship *San Felipe*, which was carrying timber, and seven men were killed. On the same day RAF Penrhos on the Lleyn peninsula came under threat. A German bomber carried out a bombing attack and flew low over the base and machine-gunned stationary aircraft. Two officers were killed, two planes were destroyed and part of the officers' quarters and a hangar were demolished.

Throughout the war there were no sustained air attacks on Anglesey and Caernarvonshire, although stragglers from raids on Liverpool sometimes jettisoned their loads randomly, killing unfortunate individuals who were in the wrong place at the wrong time and caused damage to property. Holyhead received the attentions of the Luftwaffe on a number of occasions and RAF Penrhos was attacked five times with the first attack being the most serious. Why Penrhos was targeted has been the subject of some debate. The airfield had come to prominence, both within and outside of Britain, when it was the scene of Welsh Nationalist protest in September 1936. It is likely that German intelligence over-estimated the airfield's importance because of the great amount of publicity that surrounded that the incident and subsequent trials.

After the attacks on Cardiff docks and Penrhos, Swansea docks became the victim of attack on the following day, 10 July. Eleven workmen were killed and thirty more were injured. From July 1940 until the end of May 1943 the possibility of air attack became an part of everyday life. These attacks were the precursors of greater tragedies.

The night of 14 August proved to be an eventful one in north-east Wales. Three German aircraft set out from Rennes in France under orders to attack RAF Sealand, which was an important training centre for pilots. One of the planes was shot down near the Dorset coast and another was so badly damaged that it turned back. The third continued on its mission. It reached Sealand at 10.30pm and dropped eight high explosive bombs. An officer was killed and twenty-five airmen were injured. On hearing the attack three armed Spitfires based at nearby RAF Hawarden took to the air. They each made hits against the German aircraft and it was forced to make a belly landing in the fields of Border House Farm, close to the airfield. The crew escaped from their crippled plane and then set fire to it by dropping a flare in the fuel tank. A member of the local Home Guard armed with a shotgun and the farmer took them into custody.

On 19 August and the days subsequent, dramatic events unfolded at the oil terminal at Pembroke Dock in West Wales. At 3.15am on 19 August a lone German bomber attacked the Royal Naval fuel depot at Llanreath, near Pembroke Dock, where there were seventeen massive storage tanks. The bomber scored a direct hit on one of the tanks. This started a fire that was to burn for three weeks, destroy eleven of the tanks and millions of gallons of oil. The fire was fought by approximately 650 men from twenty-two fire brigades from most parts of Wales and from as far away as Bristol and Birmingham. As the firemen tackled the fires they had to contend with four further air raids during which they were subjected to machine-gunning as well as bombing. On 22 August five Cardiff fire-fighters were killed when one of the oil tanks burst. They were engulfed by the flames which shot out from the burning tank. In addition to these deaths hundreds of others suffered from burns to the hands and face.

The firemen worked for up to nineteen hours a day in their efforts to bring the fire under control and there were many individual acts of courage as they confronted both the terrible heat and the German raid-ers. After the event thirteen firemen were awarded the George Medal, which had been introduced in September 1940 to recognise acts of heroism by civilians. The thirteen included the chief officer of Milford Haven Fire Brigade, three Cardiff firemen, eight Bristol firemen and one from Birmingham.

In terms of military impact the attack on the Pembroke Dock refineries was probably the greatest German success in Wales during the war, substantially reducing vital oil supplies. Thirty-eight million gallons were lost out of a total of forty-five million. On the other hand the firefighters' achievement in saving six of the seventeen tanks was both remarkable and heroic.

As August 1940 came to an end north-east Wales suffered its greatest loss of life from air raids. On 30 August two elderly ladies were killed in Gresford when their house was hit, and six people died and five were injured when a delayed action bomb exploded while they were looking at the wreckage. One man, three women and children were injured in Flintshire on the same night. On 31 August, eleven people died in the villages of Rhos and Penycae, near Wrexham, and extensive damage was done to property in Brymbo. During this period Liverpool was also attacked and may have been the intended target. On the other hand the raids may have been targeting steelworks and munitions factories in the area. Bombs also fell on Minera Mountain and started an extensive fire. Twenty-eight square miles of moorland between Llangollen and Ruabon were destroyed.

The next night saw the forerunner of the Nazi campaign, which has become known as the Blitz. Swansea was the focus of attack. On 24 August some German pilots failed to find their targets, an aircraft factory and an oil refinery near London. Instead they decided to drop their bombs on East End suburbs causing a large number of civilian deaths. The following night, Churchill ordered a reprisal attack on Berlin. Hitler decided to respond in kind. He ordered a change of tactics. Air attacks were now to concentrate on the British cities with the aim of destroying the morale of the civilian population. A trial run took place on 1 September. Until then attacks on cities had been made by single or small groups of planes. The Swansea raid involved a force of seventy bombers. Not only did they drop their bombs, but they repeated the tactics employed during the Pembroke Dock fire of sweeping back over their targets and machine-gunning rescue workers. Thirty-three people were killed. Six days later 600 bombers attacked London and were responsible for over 400 deaths and untold destruction. The Blitz had begun.

Initially the main target of the campaign was London, but other British cities were also in the firing line. Both Cardiff and Swansea were to suffer dreadful nights of death and destruction. Small scale attacks continued along the south coast of Wales throughout the remaining months of 1940. Several of these raids resulted in further civilian deaths. Other major towns in Britain were also subjected to the new Nazi tactics, most notoriously Coventry. At the start of the New Year, 1941, it was the turn of Cardiff. At 6.27pm on the evening of Thursday 2 January, 111 German planes began to drop flares and incendiary bombs over the city, which, according to one witness, 'gave off an eerie green light to illuminate their targets'. It was a bitterly cold, clear, moonlit night. The all clear did not sound for another ten-and-a-half hours. During this time 115 tons of high explosives were dropped, 156 people were killed and 427 were seriously injured, of whom 15 were to die later. Many houses were totally destroyed and over 600 became uninhabitable. Amongst the tragedies of that night were the deaths of over thirty people seeking safety in a private shelter beneath a bakery and a group of people attending a wake. Prominent city landmarks were hit including Llandaff Cathedral and the Arms Park rugby ground which both suffered considerable damage.

Real damage was done to the city's infrastructure. A gasworks was hit and throughout the city there were broken gas mains and water pipes plus extensive disruption to electricity supplies. Families had to be evacuated to other parts of the city to be cared for in halls converted into reception centres. Twenty-four schools were damaged and the raid finally persuaded the authorities that Cardiff should have a planned evacuation scheme for its children.

The early months of 1941 were as devastating for Swansea as they were for Cardiff. The town had suffered two serious attacks in 1940, including when it had been chosen by the Germans for a 'dummy run' for a blitz-type attack. 1941 brought new horrors, in particular, the infamous 'three nights blitz' of 19–21 February.

Swansea had already suffered serious bombing on the night of 17/18 January when the target was the docks and fifty-five people were killed. The Assistant Dock Master, Captain Luen, who was in charge of the fire service, was awarded the MBE for his work during this raid. However it was the raids on the three consecutive nights in February that totally changed the face of Swansea. The town centre was destroyed, including the market, 395 shops, offices, industrial buildings, schools, churches and chapels, a cinema, an eye hospital and a maternity home. 282 homes were completely destroyed and a further 11,000 were damaged; 232

people were killed and over 400 were injured. Amongst the dead were three firemen, three air raid wardens and four other rescue workers.

The devastation brought chaos. Hundreds of craters were created, as sewers, water pipes, gas mains and electricity supplies were put out of action and many roads became impassable. Firemen managed to get the fires under control by dawn on the first two nights of the attack but the shortage of water had a big impact on the third night and they could only watch as buildings burned themselves out. Over 6,000 people were made homeless and were fed with the help of mobile canteens and the establishment of two special cafes. Over sixty rest centres were provided. Water tankers circulated the inhabited areas distributing much needed supplies.

In 1988 the local Swansea evening newspaper asked its readers to send in stories of the 'three nights blitz'. Hundreds of stories were told and they were later published in a booklet. These letters provide an important record of those nights, including acts of individual and collective bravery. One correspondent wrote of her experience in a cinema on the second night of the attack. She had gone there, thinking that it was unlikely that air raids would take place on successive nights. When the sirens sounded the audience stayed in the cinema together and kept up their morale by singing as the bombs fell around them.

The extracts that follow from one letter help to bring alive what it must have like to live through those few days.

> The alert would moan like a wail out of hell and everyone would run for cover. Many a time bombs fell before you could reach shelter ... Oxford Street was a shambles, windows blown out, all the merchandising shattered over the road, yet nobody picked a thing up ... Everyone would come out of their shelters at dawn, only too glad to be alive. They were begrimed and dead tired, but all ready to make it to work ... Pubs were bursting at their sides even if they didn't have much to offer in the way of drinks. People just liked to get together. Sad stories and narrow escapes were an everyday experience.

One lady told the story of how her family escaped from a bombed out home whilst some near neighbours died. She described how she, her six-month-old son wrapped in a shawl, her two-year-old daughter, her younger sister and an elderly next door neighbour all crouched into a cubby hole under the stairs.

We kept very quiet, listening to the planes and shooting in the sky. Suddenly we heard a bomb whistling down. It seemed very near and there was a loud explosion. All the lights went out and the Welsh dresser crashed to the floor. The windows smashed and we could hear buildings around us falling.

We tried to get out of the pantry, but the door was blocked by rubble. We could hear people running and screaming. We stayed trapped for quite a while. Eventually we heard voices calling. We shouted back.

Our rescuers were members of the Salvation Army with hot drinks and candles for us. We cuddled together in the shattered kitchen until daylight.

It was the house next-door-but-one that had had a direct hit. There was nothing left of it, just a smouldering mass of rubble.

The people who lived in the house were a mother who was pregnant, a grandmother and a little girl (not very old).

While the men were inspecting the damage a faint cry was heard coming from under the rubble. There was a mad rush for spades or anything to dig with.

Everyone worked like Trojans to clear the debris. The three people were uncovered, but sadly the young mother-to-be and the grandmother were dead, but the little girl was still alive.

This letter in the *Evening Post* received a response a few days later, 'I was that child buried alive'. Over forty years later 'the little girl' told her story. She had been buried for fourteen hours. Bomb blasts and shock took away her sight and she was blind for about six weeks. She spent four months in hospital getting over her wounds which were mainly to her head. Her father had escaped the attack because he had been working on the night shift in a factory.

The Blitz continued from February until July. On 3 March there were fifty-one further deaths in Cardiff as over sixty tons of bombs were dropped. The Blind Institute was destroyed and the roof of St David's Cathedral. A group of children using the cathedral as a place of sanctuary were led to safety by one of the priests. The Chief Constable of Cardiff doubted that 'any town has had more incendiary bombs showered upon it in one air raid. It was a real pyrotechnic display.'

On 19 March the King and Queen visited Cardiff and Swansea and a few weeks later, in early April, Churchill followed them. There was, however, no respite from the bombing. On 15 April thirteen airmen were killed at Carew Cheriton RAF airfield in Pembrokeshire. On 29 April the South Wales coalfield suffered its most serious air raid when Cwmparc, a small village in the upper Rhondda valley, was attacked.

It is unclear why Cwmparc was a target. It has been suggested that the bombers had overshot Cardiff and had unloaded their bombs before returning to France. Twenty-seven people were killed including three evacuee children and their mother from the Manor Park area of London. These children were the victims of a terrible coincidence. They had previously stayed in a house that was hit by a bomb and had moved to another one for safety. This house was then demolished when hit by another bomb and they died in the explosion. A nurse and a special constable were also killed in this incident.

On the following night, 30 April, Cardiff faced another devastating attack. Forty-one people died. Particularly poignant on this night was the death of all ten members of one family; mother, father and eight children. The mother and seven of the children were seeking refuge in their Anderson shelter when a parachute mine fell into their back garden and exploded. The father and eldest son who were fire-watching close by also died in the resulting conflagration. Many others in their street were trapped in rubble and debris, and rescue workers toiled for hours to free them.

On 21 May the German bombers revisited Pembroke Dock. This time it was the town itself that was struck, not the oil installation. Thirty-three people died and twenty-one were seriously injured. A large number died while sheltering in the basement of a hotel. The town was targeted again on 11 June when another person was killed and on the same night a bomb killed four members of the same family in a house at Neyland several miles away.

The final attack of this phase of the air war was on Newport, the third major Welsh port on the Bristol Channel. Newport had already received visits from the Luftwaffe and there had been casualties on a number of occasions. However the night of 1 July 1941 was to be the town's worst night of the war. Thirty-seven people died, including thirty who were killed in one street as the result of one bomb.

This phase of the air war over Britain came to an end in July 1941 when a large amount of German resources were redirected towards the impending invasion of Russia. Sporadic attacks still took place across

South Wales. Although they were never again on the same scale they still had devastating consequences. People could not feel entirely safe.

In October 1941 eleven people were killed in the village of Rogerstone, just north of Newport. Deaths occurred in Cardiff following raids in July and August 1942. Then on the night of 16 February 1943 the bombers returned to Swansea. This unexpected attack, almost exactly two years after the 'three nights blitz', claimed the lives of another thirty-four people. During the raid the hospital was hit and the decision was made to evacuate 300 patients. They were moved through piles of debris, with no lighting and the added danger of escaping gas. This was Swansea's last attack, but further raids were made on Cardiff in March and May 1943. On 18 May the last raid on Wales took place. Sixty high explosive bombs were dropped and forty-one people were killed. The targets were probably the American troops stationed in the city, the Royal Ordnance Factory at Llanishen, railway lines and the Docks. For the first time in the war the Germans were successful in hitting the steelworks.

When the all-clear sounded at 3.59am on that day it marked the end of the German offensive against Wales. Mercifully Wales was out of range from the last air campaign against Britain involving the V1 and the V2 rockets, making it a safe area to host another wave of evacuees. The German air war over Wales claimed 985 lives, including 387 in Swansea and 355 in Cardiff. The tragedy of the civilian casualties of these air raids is the only example in modern times of Welsh people falling victim to the aggressive intentions of an enemy on home soil.

Remarkably, despite having taken reconnaissance pictures of important munitions factories, airfields and steelworks, apart from the inferno at Pembroke Dock – which cost millions of gallons of oil – very little material damage was done to essential war industry. On the other hand the air war caused massive destruction to the town centre of Swansea, so that it had to be virtually rebuilt, and the demolition of a great deal of homes and properties in Cardiff.

## The Fall of France and the South Wales Coalfield

The build up to and the outbreak of war had brought prospects of greater economic security for the Welsh coal industry. Throughout 1939 there was a steady decline in unemployment. By August 1939 the number of unemployed miners had halved compared with August 1938. Four months into the war a new industrial era was being heralded for Wales. The impetus stemmed from the increased production required from staple industries such as coal and steel alongside the influx of secondary industries into the region.

The benefits of a location away from those parts of Britain most likely to take the brunt of the first enemy onslaughts became quickly apparent. The chairman of Abertillery Chamber of Commerce reported in October 1939 that 'activities at the collieries have been growing and without saying anything of the merits or demerits of the war, that is surely one thing we have to be thankful for'.

The military situation on the continent created new markets for the coal trade. Competition from Germany and Poland was removed and other countries experiencing a shortage of supplies were driven to buy from Britain. The greatest demand of all came from France as the country strove to build its defences against the potential of a German invasion. Demand accelerated after March 1940 when the French Prime Minister appealed to his British counterpart, Neville Chamberlain, for his country's requirements to be given priority. French coal stocks needed to be rebuilt with British imports and a large percentage was to come from the South Wales coalfield.

The period from March to June was to be a hectic one in the coal industry as efforts were made to try and meet the demand. Whilst this was a period of almost total quiescence in terms of industrial disputes, the production drive did serve to reopen a number of old scars, for example the debate over pit closures. The most serious problem, however, was that the maximum production of coal was being impeded by a lack of manpower. Mining had not been made a reserved occupation, thus 12,000 Welsh colliers had joined the armed forces, and the majority of these were young workers who would have been working at the coal-face. Others had drifted from the industry into the new armaments factories. Many of the unemployed miners coming back to work were older men who were not fit to work at the face and having been unemployed for years were unused to new techniques of mechanisation. The miners union, the SWMF, called for the recruitment of miners into the armed forces to be stopped and for miners to be prevented from leaving the pits for other government work; in May 1940 the government responded by passing the appropriate legislation.

Whilst these debates were taking place events in the theatre of war were accelerating at a frightening rate. Hitler's invasion of Belgium and Holland somewhat invalidated long-term solutions to the production problem such as the reopening of pits. The burden, inevitably, fell on the miner at the point of production. Only his extra efforts could deliver the goods. The output of saleable coal and the individual output per man employed were both the highest for the April to June 1940 quarter than for any other quarter during the war years. The Industrial Relations Officer for South Wales wrote on 1 June 1940 that

> The grave news from overseas has united all parties in industry in grim determination to do everything possible to enable the government to continue the war effectively. Realisation of the seriousness of the situation has raised, rather than depressed the morale of the workers.

In the months from the outbreak of the war until June 1940 the drive for increased coal production totally preoccupied the coal industry. They were months of frenetic activity. Argument and debate were ongoing on a range of issues such as pit closures, manpower shortages, wages, the length of the working day and holidays, but the effort to produce the coal with the available workforce was incessant. On 15 June a special conference of the SWMF unanimously accepted measures, such as an additional Sunday shift, designed to increase production. Days later France was out of the war, the demand for extra coal was gone and new disasters were foreseen. On 25 June a *Daily Herald* reporter wrote:

> Wales has been severely hit by the French capitulation. Between 80% and 90% of its coal trade has come to a standstill. 'France First' has been the watchword in Wales for coal supplies since the war started. Other markets have been neglected so that our Ally could be supplied. Wales is paying dearly for its loyalty.

As evacuated soldiers returned with the remains of the BEF from Dunkirk and the first air raid sirens were heard in Britain's cities, Wales was to suffer 'the indirect consequences of the Blitzkreig' as the 'bubble' of war prosperity burst. Collieries were to close down and miners were to trudge back to the unemployment queues or face transference to work in other parts of the country. The Fall of France and the entrance of

Italy into the war on Hitler's side meant that the South Wales coal trade lost its two major export markets. By the end of July 1940 forty-three pits were wholly idle and nine more were partly closed. In November 1940, at a time when the British people faced its gravest threat from an invading force for centuries, the ghosts of the depression revisited the South Wales coalfield as nearly 96,000 people collected their dole.

When France signed its armistice with Hitler, there was 1,500,000 tons of Welsh coal in transit. This coal had to return to the Bristol Channel ports. In addition there were thousands of tons being held at collieries as stock. The South Wales collieries were being 'choked' with their own output because the coal was not being taken away. At the same time a transport crisis had developed that cut off South Wales from its inland markets as well as its export markets.

The area west of Port Talbot, including the Neath, Swansea, Gwendraeth and Amman Valleys was most affected. Railway sidings were full with stationary wagons full of coal awaiting delivery. In November, one combine in the Neath Valley reported that only one of its five collieries was working. Seventy-five per cent of the workforce – 2,500 men – were unemployed. This was attributed to the failure of the railway companies to affect transport clearance owing to appalling congestion. In the Gwendraeth Valley there were 6,000 wagons loaded with coal intended for the French and Italian markets.

Several wartime measures necessitated by the French collapse and Nazi air raids had an affect on freight transportation. Freight carried on the east coast railways was largely diverted to western routes as air raids interrupted rail travel and damage to lines required alternative planning of routes. There was a shortage of rail staff and an increase in general traffic such as munitions and civilian evacuees. The coal transport problem was made worse in South Wales because of a bottleneck that existed at the Severn Tunnel which was not addressed until the early months of 1941; it was eventually resolved by stopping maintenance work that was usually carried out on Sundays and reducing passenger traffic between London and South Wales.

In addition to the rail problems, sea freight was restricted by the withdrawal of Royal Navy destroyers from convoy duties, and difficulties were created as the docks in Cardiff and Swansea became prime targets for enemy attacks. Road haulage was restricted too, because of the withdrawal of men and lorries for military service.

One of the greatest ironies of the situation was that as the coal remained in the sidings at South Wales' railway stations, elsewhere in the country there were shortages. In early November supplies of coal to households in south-east England were rationed.

Bert Coombes kept a diary during this period:

> ... we see men fetching their tools home from work every day now ... Also I see men, women and children scratching for coal in the tips whilst the rain is freezing on them. Facing me, as I write is a mountain so full of coal that it crops out to the surface. Yet the people have empty grates.

The crisis reopened old political arguments and the question of nationalisation of the coal industry returned to the agenda, especially as the perception was that it was the workers in the industry who were bearing the brunt of the problems rather than the owners.

It is difficult, however, not to agree with the MP for Aberdare, George Hall when he told a public meeting that

> No provision could wholly have protected us from the devastating effects of such losses [the coal trade with Italy and France]. They must be regarded as amongst the incalculable hazards of war and as unforeseen contingencies created by Hitler's initial success.

Between the end of June 1940 and December 1940 unemployment increased in South Wales by nearly 30,000. Particular areas of the coalfield were affected. These were the West Wales anthracite coalfield and the Aberdare and Rhondda Valleys. In the Rhondda Valley only four out of eighteen pits were working to full capacity in November 1940.

Councillor Frank Davies of Ammanford told the 'People's Convention' in London in January 1941 that in an orbit of five miles of the town there were at least 3,000 miners who were unemployed. Ammanford is approximately ten miles to the north west of Swansea which was the target of Nazi bombers throughout this period. In the week before Christmas 1940 only seven collieries, out of thirty-three in the Amalgamated Anthracite Company, worked; 12,000 men were laid off.

The position in the West Wales coalfield, centred on the towns of Llanelli and Ammanford, was particularly bleak given that the other major staple industry in the area – tin-plate – was also faced with closures. This was partly due to the opening of the large steel works in Ebbw Vale in 1938. It was not surprising therefore that a town like Ammanford had a strong People's Vigilance Committee as the suffering caused by the dislocation of trade was as intense as it was familiar. Despite the recognition of the need to accept the situation of late 1940 in the interests of patriotism, the memory of past industrial conflict was never far from the surface.

The pace of events surrounding the Fall of France and consequent need to protect cities and towns from air raids and to prepare against the imminent fear of invasion created a complexity of circumstances that made decision making extremely exacting. The sudden reversal of the fortunes of the South Wales coal trade found the government entangled in the mesh of its own legislation. In May 1940 – at a time when every muscle and sinew was being stretched to boost coal production – it had been decided to stop the recruitment of miners into the armed services and factories. Six weeks later thousands of miners were paralysed in a state of unemployment as they were not allowed to search for alternative work. Workers from the border areas of England were being brought to work in the munitions factories of Wales whilst the locally unemployed miners were not allowed to work there.

Ernest Bevin, the Minister of Labour lifted the restrictions in September 1940 under pressure from miners' leaders. He announced that substantial numbers of miners from the lower age groups were to be called-up into military service. It was a decision he was to bitterly regret later in the war when the problem of the shortage of mineworkers was to become one of the most intractable problems of labour supply that he had to address.

In addition to the reintroduction of military call-up for miners the government proposed that others could be transferred to other work through the labour exchanges. For example twenty-five men from the Gwaun-cae-Gurwen area were recruited to build an aerodrome in the south-west of England. The scheme was not popular given that there was an element of compulsion. It was impossible for a man to refuse to take the work because of an amendment to the Unemployed Insurance Act in the early days of the war. The extent of migration from the villages of the West Wales coalfield was high. In April 1941 representatives on Ammanford Trades Council estimated that only 100 men out of a workforce of 500 at Pantyffynon Colliery were left in the area. Of the

316 men who had worked at the Saron Colliery only fifty were left. The local newspaper, the *Llanelly Star* expressed its fears for the future of the communities:

> The coal-mining industry seems to be fated to be the orphan of every storm. And the South Wales coalfield always gets its worst. Our dependence on the export market renders us victims of every international crisis ... The Government is surely under obligation to do something for stricken communities. They are the casualties of war.

The crisis in the coal industry began to ease in the early months of 1941 but its impact had significant long term effects. The wartime history of the coal industry became dominated by one factor – the failure to achieve adequate production to meet the wartime needs. By 1945 coal production was between thirty and forty million tons below the pre-war level. Initially, the building up of stocks after the Fall of France helped to delay the effects of the severe shortage of production, but the events surrounding the Fall of France, such as the release of colliers to join the armed forces, were instrumental in creating the shortage.

On 28 May 1941 the Secretary of State for the Mines informed the House of Commons that the rate of coal output at that time was insufficient to meet the needs of the country. Weekly production was at least 1,000 tons below national consumption. At this time wartime factory production was beginning to operate at full capacity.

This statement astounded many. Not only the thousands of miners who had found themselves unemployed during the previous winter, but learned journals such as *The Economist*. From this point on, however, the crisis deepened on an annual basis. British coal production fell each year throughout the war, presenting a phenomenon described by Professor W.H.B. Court as 'One of the most remarkable features of the economic history of the war'. The phenomenon was common to all British coalfields, but it was particularly accentuated in South Wales. In 1943 the annual production figure for the South Wales coalfield was the lowest recorded for over sixty years and it fell again in both 1944 and 1945.

The most direct cause of the decline in output was the shortage of men working in the pits. In 1944 there were nearly 19,000 fewer men employed in the mines of South Wales compared with 1939. There were two significant periods when manpower dropped. As previously discussed, the first was in the months just prior to the start of the war and in the early months of the war when there was a period of considerable unrestricted recruitment into the armed forces. The major drop was in the months following the Fall of France. 16,404 less men worked in the industry in 1941 as compared to 1940 – ninety per cent of the wartime decline was accounted for by the migration of men from the industry as a direct result of the Fall of France.

In May 1941 the government applied the Essential Works Order (Coalmining Industry) that restricted the recruitment of miners to the armed forces and factories. Within twelve months events had turned a full circle.

The events surrounding the Fall of France were to have an adverse effect on the morale of the workforce. By the middle of 1942 there was a general crisis across all industries related to production. A mass observation survey at the time considered that a major force militating towards a decline in British war production was low morale. A House of Commons select committee on expenditure that examined the experiences of miners in these months reported that the

> … consequent psychological effect on the miners of the absence of any measure to meet the sudden change in demand was deplorable, as at one moment they were urged to produce as much as possible and the next they found themselves without work.

There was also anger in some quarters at what was considered to be an inequality of sacrifice. Ned Gittens – a correspondent for the *Merthyr Express* – complained that during the two crises before and after the Fall of France the government asked sacrifices of the miners but never the owners. Miners had been expected to work extra shifts before the Fall of France and then afterwards they were expected to transfer to alternative work in other areas of the country. At the same time the government assisted the coal owners by increasing the price of coal by one shilling and nine pence a ton.

There is little doubt that during this period Labour Party political activists and trade union leaders were provided with substantial evidence to support their proposal that the coal industry should be nationalised. It was to be a significant component of the Labour Party Manifesto in the 1945 General Election.

# Chapter Four

# Wartime Changes – Air Raid Precautions, Rationing and Women at Work

## Air-Raid Precautions

The war was to change the daily life of every individual in the country, both because of the preparations made to defend the country from invasion and the direct consequences of the conflict itself.

Critics of the pre-war government accused it of inadequacy in the making of effective preparations for the eventuality of conflict. It is somewhat surprising, therefore, to find that as early as July 1935 local authorities were being urged to create plans for precautions in case of air raids. Real measures, however, did not begin until 1937 when councils in Wales began to set up air raid precaution committees. The response was mixed and it was not until the early months of 1938 – with the emerging crisis over the Nazi claims that the Sudetenland should be incorporated into the German state – that the recruitment of air raid wardens and other activities related to air raid precautions gathered momentum. A thirty-six page booklet on protecting homes against air raids was distributed to all domestic residences.

On 28 September 1938 all the head teachers in Cardiff were summoned to a meeting on air raid precautions and on the next day the distribution of gas masks began. The large cities were presumably given priority as the gas masks in the town of Pontypridd did not arrive until April 1939. The issue of gas masks was the government response to the fear that poisonous gas would be dropped on the civilian population by the enemy during aerial bombardment. Soon, evacuation drill and the wearing of gas masks became a part of the school curriculum across the country. On 19 October 1938 a mock air raid took place over Cardiff.

In July 1939 the Civil Defence Act gave local authorities the powers to build public air raid shelters and required all employers to set up ARP training schemes. Across the country trenches were dug in local parks, thousands of sandbags were filled for the purpose of protecting public buildings against incendiary bombs and a programme for the building of public shelters was begun. The trenches were designed to act as primitive air raid shelters in city and town centres. They were to be covered with corrugated iron sheets in the case of an air raid. Nine miles of trenches were dug across Cardiff. The trenches built in the town of Caerphilly had become water-logged by December 1939 and were a danger to the public.

Cardiff City Council appears to have been fairly effective in developing its shelter programme. The basements of many buildings were strengthened and 220 shelters were built. Provision was made to shelter 2,500 people beneath the walls of Cardiff Castle. Including the distribution of 22,000 Anderson shelters it was estimated that there were 155,000 places in shelters across the city. In Swansea, the story was not so good. A report in 1948 on Swansea's preparations for war stated that by the time that the air raids began, basements in public buildings and crypts in churches and chapels were the main type of public shelter. In February 1940 6,549 Anderson shelters had been delivered to the town when it was estimated that 30,000 were needed. The westerly location of the city may have been a factor in the delay and, of course, the consequences of the Fall of France were not anticipated.

Public shelters were built in most towns and all businesses and factories employing over fifty people had to have an air raid shelter. The public shelters were usually windowless brick buildings with reinforced concrete roofs. They were unpleasant places that became associated with the smell of damp urine. In some places they were vandalised.

Homeowners with gardens could obtain Anderson shelters. Six foot high, five foot wide and six foot long, they were sunk into the ground. They were designed to protect six people and were safe except in the case of a direct hit. Despite the shelters being cold and flooding after heavy rain, many people in Cardiff and Swansea owed their lives to them.

Some people created their own shelters and large numbers went under the stairs, or into cellars and basements.

In the early months of 1939 the Air Raid Warden Service was set up. Some wardens were employed full-time but the majority were part-time and unpaid. Cardiff City Council was authorised to pay 500 full-time wardens but never found it necessary to appoint more than forty-five. By May 1940 there were 4,000 volunteers. When another 1,500 were required once the air raids began this number was quickly achieved. Their duties were to advise people about the location of local shelters and assist them there, report the fall of bombs and any fires in their sector, check on damage, and guide the police and fire brigade to incidents. Once air raids began their knowledge of which families lived in each house was important in determining if occupants had made it to a public shelter or if they were still in their homes.

The job was a frontline occupation and members of the service were killed in the line of duty in both Cardiff and Swansea. In 1988 Mrs Eva Ridler recalled the work of her father during the Swansea air raids. She remembered that when the rest of the family went into their shelter he could not stay because he was an air raid warden. 'It was a relief when the "All Clear" would sound and he would come home safe.' She described how, during one air raid he and her brother once rushed into a house and brought out a blazing bed. Fortunately, the old lady who lived in the house had gone to the shelter.

All the wardens had a dangerous job and they saw a lot of terrible things going on around them and no matter how bad things were they still had to cope. So, we should always be proud and remember the ARP wardens … They were always around when they were needed.

Outside of the large towns the majority of wardens were not called upon to fulfil their intended function. Their role became most closely associated with policing the blackout, a role that did not always make them popular. The blackout officially began on Friday 1 September 1939, two days before the actual declaration of war. Strict regulations were to remain in place until September 1944 when they were eased. To the outside world homes, businesses, factories and roads had to appear in complete darkness between sunrise and sunset. Gas and electrical street lighting was extinguished and every household fitted black screens or heavy curtains over their doors and windows. In addition homeowners were advised to put sticky tape across their windows to reduce the danger from the splintering of glass in the case of an explosion. Factories and other large buildings were painted in black, brown or dark green to reduce their usage as land marks for enemy bombers.

The blackout created dangers in itself and there were many casualties, including deaths as a result of its application. These were mainly road deaths. In the environs of Pontypridd, for example, a pensioner and an eight-year-old boy were both killed in October 1939 as a result of accidents caused by blackout restrictions. Initially, cars were required to drive without any lights at all. Eventually kerbs, trees and lamp posts were decorated with daubs of white paint to help people find their way in the dark and the lights on cars were fitted with special hooded masks with slits. Accidents at sea were also put down to the existence of the blackout and the removal of navigational aids associated with it. At the end of 1940 two ships ran aground off the coast of Anglesey and their crews were rescued by coastguards from Holyhead. In 1943 the liner *Castillian* sailed into the Skerries, a series of rocky islets off the north-west coast of Anglesey. The Holyhead lifeboat service came to the rescue again. In the Bristol Channel there were several collisions between vessels.

The blackout was one of those features of wartime that became custom but at the same time contributed to the draining of human resources. Everyone was affected, but in particular those who worked on early and late shifts in mines and factories. This extract from the diary of miner Bert Coombes provides a graphic description.

> It is a terrible job going to work these nights of black velvet. The buses creep into the colliery area like great glow-worms carrying only the faintest light in front. After we leave the baths we have no light of any sort to guide us up the mountain incline ... A flooding river splashes far below on our right and a line of whitened posts mark the danger edge of the ravine ... The crowd of men stumble on through the darkness ... They touch one another so that they shall have guidance. When one kicks an obstruction he warns the others, when someone falls down hands shoot out to help him swiftly to his feet.

The breaking of blackout regulations created new illegal practices. Fines were imposed on people whose homes were not properly blacked out.

They were liable to a £50 fine, but in most cases it was around ten shillings. It was the job of air raid wardens to check that no chink of light could be seen from the outside of houses. Local newspapers from the period provide many examples of prosecutions. Most people abided by the regulations and often if wardens saw some light they would bang on the door and tell the occupants to cover up the offending area. Some wardens, however, were over zealous in pursuing prosecutions and this led to their unpopularity in some quarters. They were accused of behaving like mini-dictators. Don Powell in his history of Pontypridd at war describes one case where prosecution seemed to be unwarranted. A woman from Cilfynydd was fined ten shillings for allowing the light from a candle to flicker momentarily in the small panes of her front door as she shepherded her children to bed after sheltering under the stairs. She told the magistrate that he should be with her husband 'missing in the jungle with the Japs'. On the other hand there were some individuals that flouted the regulations deliberately. A case in point was that of two sisters, British but of Italian parentage, from Port Talbot who were members of the Italian Fascist Party. They were prosecuted on three occasions for contravention of blackout regulations.

As the war progressed the danger of aerial bombardment became more remote and war-weariness became an increasing factor affecting the efficiency of the workforce. At the same time attitudes to wartime regulations started to become more negative. In August 1943 the lack of sensitivity in policing the regulations was cited as a contributory cause to the developing unrest amongst miners in the South Wales coalfield. At the Lewis Merthyr Colliery, near Bedlinog, men had been told by an official to carry lights for a particular job that were deemed by the police to be beyond what was necessary. The men were fined for an offence against the lighting regulations. What was odd about the case was that it was the men who were fined and not the colliery company at whose behest the men had carried the lights. In September 1944 there was a considerable relaxing in the regulations and on 24 April 1945 they were abolished.

On 14 May 1940, in the wake of the Nazi invasion of Belgium and Holland the British government announced the establishment of a civilian defence organisation. Originally known as the Local Defence Volunteers it became more famous as the Home Guard. Within twenty-four hours there were 250,000 volunteers and by the end of June there were 1,500,000. In Llandudno, for example, 200 men volunteered on the day of the announcement, followed by a further 500 in the following weeks. Nearly half of those who joined in this initial phase had fought in the previous war, older men who were above the age limit for conscription and were under the age of sixty-five. The others were young men between the age of sixteen and eighteen and men working in reserved occupations. Grafton Maggs, a young member of the Home Guard in Mumbles described the make up of his local unit:

> It was obvious from the start that there were factions – the Great War warriors and the raw youngsters. Old soldiers passed on a wealth of experience to lads like me.
>
> The Company was a wonderful melting pot. Village lads rubbed shoulders with residents of Langland and Caswell (more affluent areas). Solicitor stood by dustman, company bosses by men from the factory floor. Social barriers were broken down, as never before – it was a delightful period of warmth and great friendship.

In the early months of its existence the Home Guard was seriously lacking in equipment. Glyndwr Jones from Caerphilly has written that the weapons were mainly shotguns from farmers. In October 1941 some units were issued with pikes – 3 foot 6 inch long gas pipes with 18 inches of bayonet stuck in the end. Rifle drills were usually carried out with broom handles.

The role of the Home Guard, in preparation for invasion, was to practise rifle shooting and the throwing of homemade grenades on ranges, building and manning roadblocks in case German parachutists dropped, and preparing for fire fighting. At the Mumbles, and other coastal locations, they supported the Royal Artillery in the manning of anti-aircraft guns.

Their activities were not always popular, illustrated by this remembrance from a resident of Carmarthen.

> The Home Guard caused my grandfather great inconvenience, because all they seemed to do was set up checkpoints on the outskirts of Carmarthen town, a mass of sandbags that reduced the road to half-width, so they could stop every car and search it for spies and fifth columnists. My grandfather was neither, he was a farmer.

In Bettws-y-Coed a more serious incident took place when a doctor was shot in the chest at a roadblock.

In Cardiff and Swansea the Home Guard played a significant support role during the periods of the Blitz. In other parts of the country there was less need for active engagement. Some units became involved when there was a plane crash in their vicinity. However, during 1940 through to the early months of 1942 there was a need for constant prepared-ness and vigilance. The summer of 1940 was a time of particular tension following the retreat from Dunkirk, the beginning of the German air attacks and the fear that invasion was imminent. This was the main period of roadblock activity. In May 1940 all road signs were removed and churches were prevented from ringing their bells. If church bells were to ring it was the warning that invasion had begun.

On the evening of the 7 September 1940 the London Blitz began. The Chief of Staff issued the codeword 'Cromwell', which was to sig-nify 'invasion' to army commanders across the country. Unofficially the Home Guard became aware of the alert. In Llandudno the Home Guard were called out and ordered to their battle stations at the town hall, on the sea front and on the golf links. This was replicated in many places and in some the church bells were rung. The army remained on alert for twelve days. No sea-borne invasion materialised, but London was at the beginning of a terrifying seventy-six day ordeal.

From August 1940 the Home Guard became increasingly regulated and units became affiliated to county regiments. In February 1941 ranks, as in the regular army, were introduced. All officers were reviewed and many removed from their commands. In early 1942 there was compul-sory enrolment and the emphasis was on the training of the younger element in preparation for their call-up to the regular army.

## Rationing

In addition to the distribution of gas masks, plans for shelters and the establishment of the ARP the government had made preparations for rationing, in particular petrol and food. Petrol was the first item to be rationed in September 1939. Initially the ration was on the basis of the size of the car. The owner of a small car would get four gallons a month which would enable travel of 100–200 miles, whilst the owner of a Rolls-

Royce would get ten gallons. Extra rations were available for essential users. As the war progressed supplies became more stretched, especially as German U-boats targeted oil tankers. When Japan invaded Malaya in the summer of 1942 this further reduced the supply of petrol and of rubber for tyres and led to a ban on using petrol for private purposes. Rationing led to the introduction of new crimes, such as the forging of coupons or claiming additional supplies by false pretences. The first such case was heard in a Bridgend police court in January 1940.

Petrol rationing did not have an impact on the majority of people, although the differentiation between the owners of particular types of car reinforced public attitudes that the privileges of the wealthy would not be threatened by the war. Far more people were affected by the rationing of food, introduced in response to the fear of shortages. Over half of Britain's food was imported from abroad before the start of the war with meat, sugar, fruit and tea featuring prominently. Plans came into play almost as soon as the war started and everyone was expected to register with their chosen retailers by 23 November 1939 in readiness for rationing to begin on 8 January 1940.

The first products to be rationed were bacon, ham, butter and sugar. In March 1940 meat followed. Other foodstuffs that entered the ration books included eggs, cheese, milk, tea, coffee, chocolate and sweets. Un-rationed food was price controlled and a series of regulations were introduced to ensure that fairness prevailed. Rations fluctuated due to the level of imports.

The preparations proved totally justified as within weeks of the introduction of rationing, Denmark – the source of much bacon and dairy produce – fell under German control. Once the 'phoney war' period was over and particularly after the Fall of France the Nazis intensified their strategy of starving Britain into submission via the U-boat campaign against ships carrying supplies into Britain. Their possession of the French Atlantic ports marked the beginning of the Battle of the Atlantic, 'the single longest running battle of the war'. It was a battle to which Welsh seamen and Welsh ports would make a large contribution.

Shipping was a major employer in Wales at the start of the war and the ports of Newport, Cardiff, Barry, Swansea, Milford Haven and Holyhead had an important part to play in both the receipt of imports and in the carriage of exports. Whilst most of the action in the campaign against the convoys took place hundreds of miles from Wales in the mid-Atlantic, there was significant action in the coastal waters around the country which took a heavy toll on merchant shipping and Welsh seamen.

Phil Carradine and Terry Breverton provide some remarkable statistics in their book *Welsh Sailors in the Second World War*. The Welsh merchant fleet was almost totally destroyed. Of 164 registered ships in Welsh ports 123 were damaged or destroyed during the war with a loss of life of 1,532 men. In addition thirty-three fishing boats were damaged or destroyed with a further loss of over 100 men. A study has been made of the port of Barry. At least 360 merchant seamen from the town died during the war. The Sunday newspaper *Reynolds News* stated in 1943 that 'Barry Dock, Wales' famous seaport, has lost more merchant seamen in the war than any other seaport of comparable size in Britain ... There are few streets in the town and dock area which have not lost men at sea as a result of enemy action.' The predominant cause of the sinking of ships was the German U-boats, but twenty-two were the victim of aircraft bombings and another ten hit mines.

The U-boats did not generally come close to the Welsh coast although they were active a distance away in the area between Anglesey and the Isle of Man, threatening the shipping lanes into Liverpool. In the closing months of the war, however, they became more active nearer the coast. On 10 December 1944 the *Dan Beard* was torpedoed seven miles off Strumble Head, Pembrokeshire and a motor vessel, the *King Edgar* was sunk off St David's Head on 2 March 1945. On the other hand three U-boats were sunk off the North Wales coast, one in January and the other two in May.

Most allied shipping losses that took place around the Welsh coast were due to mines dropped into the sea by enemy planes or direct aircraft attack. At least thirty merchant ships were sunk in the Bristol Channel. The indiscriminate dropping of mines and the air attacks impacted from July 1940 onwards following the Nazi seizure of airfields in France. On 22 July 1940 a trawler, the *Campina* struck a mine and sank a few hundred yards from the Holyhead lighthouse and a month later three Irish seamen on the SS *Meath* were injured when it hit a mine in the same area. A patrol boat, the *Manx Lad*, sent out to rescue her, hit another mine and sank. In the Bristol Channel fifteen men were killed when the cargo ship *The Cato* was mined off Nash Point, Glamorganshire in October 1940. The following month the *Dakotian* was sunk near Dale in

Pembrokeshire on 21 November and the steamship *Pikepool* was sunk off the same coast later in the day. The captain and crew survived on life rafts for forty-eight hours before being rescued.

A number of ships were bombed in Caernarvon Bay including an oil tanker the *Lucellum* off Bardsey Island on 19 December 1941. Six crewmen and two gunners died and the survivors reached Holyhead in their lifeboats. In the Bristol Channel at least three ships were sunk by German bombers, whilst on 13 June the cross channel ferry from Rosslare to Fishguard was struck by bombs and sunk within five minutes. Seventeen crewmen and twelve passengers were drowned, twelve miles from Fishguard.

The casualties of war around the Welsh coast would have been even greater had it not been for the efforts of rescue services. The Mumbles Lifeboat, for example was called out twenty-three times and saved 137 lives. Veteran crews came back into service as the younger men were away in the armed services. Tom Ace, a member of the lifeboat service during the war made the following contribution to the booklet *Memories of Mumbles at War.*

About 7.30 in the evening of 14 October 1944, Coxswain William Gammon came to me and said, 'Tom, there's a vessel in distress off Port Talbot.' It was blowing a 90m.p.h. gale and the official order had not come through because all the telephone lines were down. We decided to carry on and pick up the old stagers – Jolly Joe, 72 years old; Charlie 'Rum' Davies, 70; Mike, 80 and Tommy 'Russy' Davies 63. A Canadian ship had been torpedoed in the Atlantic and was being towed. She had come 1,000 miles, but by the time they were off Mumbles Roads, the tug had to leave her to save her own skin. This part of the coast is called 'Lifeboatman's Dread' ... We went round her [the *Chebogue*] 12 to 14 times and in heavy sea and wind, with every sharp parting, the 42 of them jumped on board. We got them home safely with the exception of one sailor who had broken his leg jumping.'

The coxswain, William Gammon was awarded the RNLI Gold Medal.

The experience of Welsh merchant shipping brought home the justification for rationing. As the war progressed the list of rationed foodstuffs extended. In November 1941 canned foods, meat, fish and vegetables, were rationed, in January 1942 dried fruit, rice, sago and pulses followed and in February canned fruit and tomatoes. At the same time soap was rationed. In July 1942 chocolate and sweets were rationed followed by biscuits in August and the manufacture of ice cream was made illegal in September.

Rationing was generally perceived as being fair although there were widespread feelings that the rich and middle classes did not share the privations of the rest of society to the same extent. For many, rationing was merely an extension of their pre-war experience. 'Rationing? We've been on rationing for twenty years' a housewife from Blaina, Monmouthshire, told a researcher from Mass Observation in 1942.

Megan Thomas of Newport, a child throughout the war, recalls that she never starved 'but we ate some funny things'. Foremost amongst these were dried eggs and whale meat. She also recalls that 'things kept "appearing" in our house', such as a box of Mars Bars and a seven-pound tin of butter. It never occurred to her until after the war that her father must have 'received stolen goods knowing them to have been sold from the Black Market'.

Glyndwr Jones – who has written extensively on the local history of the Caerphilly area – has noted that whilst the vast majority of people were honest 'there were some on the "fiddle" to be found in most towns'. He cites the example of a local farmer who was fined for adding 60 per cent water to his milk and a milkman who claimed subsidies for selling milk to evacuees who did not exist. These were small-scale offences; however, there were serious large-scale criminal activities that developed in response to rationing and shortages. This 'dark' side of wartime Britain has recently been revealed by Donald Thomas in his book *An Underworld at War*, published in 2003. He describes some activities that had an impact in Wales. One concerned the illegal and unsanitary manufacture of beauty products such as perfumes and eau de Cologne complete with forged labels. In the spring of 1944 Cardiff and Swansea were flooded with these bottles and the two perpetrators of the scam made £500 profit in two days. (Equivalent to £20,000 today). They had used a Cardiff railway station cloakroom to store their wares and were traced there and caught.

One of the commonest crimes was the theft of and the selling on of clothing coupons. Clothes were rationed from June 1941 using a points system, so that consumers could build up their points and have a choice of garments which they could be exchanged for. In 1944 a major coupon-trafficking case linked London and South Wales. The scheme depended on the regular theft in Cardiff of merchant navy clothing coupons from shipping offices in the docks. These were then supplied to receivers in London who sold them in hotels and public houses there. The gang were caught in July 1944.

On the other hand, when the government declared war on waste, some traditionally law-abiding individuals found themselves contravening regulations. It became illegal for example to give fresh milk to pets and to feed birds with bread that was fit for human consumption. The warden of a hostel in Bridgend was fined for sending 'perfectly wholesome' bread to a piggery, whilst a Cardiff lady was fined for feeding bread to birds, which could have been put in the bins for pig swill.

Other measures were introduced to bolster food production. Householders were encouraged to dig up their flower gardens and replace them with vegetable allotments. Municipal parks and golf courses were similarly utilised.

As part of the war on waste there was a salvage drive. People were encouraged to 'ransack' their homes for metal objects, bones and paper. The metal, including pots and pans and garden railings could be melted down to aid the production of ships, aircraft, tanks and guns. The bones could be ground down to make glue for aircraft, glycerine for explosives, feeding meal for cattle and fertilizer for the land. The paper could be repulped for newsprint and the making of boxes.

Malcolm Pill, author of *A Cardiff Family in the Forties* recalls the removal of the iron railings from the small wall at the front of his home:

> Along with all the others in Clive Street, they were burnt off and taken to be used in the war effort. This appeared to me to be a perfectly natural and routine event though the stubs left in the stonework could be a hazard. I speculated as to whether our railings would form a vital part of a warship or of a tank.

Many Welsh women had long experience of making ends meet. The conditions imposed by rationing, whilst created by different circumstances, were not beyond their ingenuity in providing for their families. The restrictions were accepted as a necessity, but as the threat of invasion receded they became less palatable, and added to the growing anti-government mood that began to develop throughout 1943.

# Women at Work

The historian Mari Williams entitled her book on female munitions workers in South Wales, 1939 – 1945, *A Forgotten Army*. By 1943 over half of those engaged in the war industry in Wales were women. Until the 1980s their role in the war effort and the impact on the role of women within Welsh society had been largely neglected. Due to the work of Mari Williams, Deidre Beddoe, Angela John and others, the imbalance of attention has received a degree of correction.

Throughout the United Kingdom the increased employment of women was a major feature of the changes wrought by war on the Home Front. No more so than in Wales. In 1923 there were eight insured women workers for every 100 men in Wales. By 1936 this figure had doubled to sixteen, but the proportion was still far below the UK average of thirty-nine to 100. Between 1939 and 1941, the first two years of the war, the ratio approached the national average.

The majority of women who were employed in the inter-war years were young people in domestic service. In the early 1930s, the worst years of the Depression, the response of many in Wales to the shortage of work was to migrate to parts of England. Twice as many females as males were to leave, mainly for work in service.

Towards the end of the 1930s the establishment of state-funded trading estates created new opportunities for work, including the use of female labour. However, of all the designated Special Areas, the percentage of women employed in Wales was the lowest. The country's dependence on heavy industry had little tradition of women working outside of the service sector and very little involvement of married women in particular.

By March 1942 more than half of all war workers in Wales were women. Between July 1939 and July 1943 the number of insured female workers had increased by 139 per cent. In the words of Mari Williams, 'in an extremely short period of time, the working experiences of the female population of Wales had undergone a bewildering transformation.' The greatest reason for the growth in female labour was the work generated by the munitions factories. Of the 50,000 workforce employed at the Glascoed and Bridgend Royal Ordnance Factories, two of the largest shell filling factories, over 70 per cent were female.

The recruitment of labour for the munitions factories and other war work began in earnest in early 1940 and accelerated later in the year following the Fall of France and the fear of imminent invasion by the Nazis. It was not until the early months of 1941 that many of the factories were ready to work to full production. However, the voluntary principle in relation to recruitment had not generated the workforce needed and labour shortages were holding up production. At the same time there was a manpower crisis in the coal industry, which led to the establishment of an Essential Works Order that in effect tied men to the industry.

In March 1941 all women between nineteen and forty-one years of age had to register at employment exchanges. Single, childless, women aged between twenty and thirty were regarded as 'mobile', which meant that they could be directed to work anywhere in Britain.

In December 1941 the government passed the National Service Act which gave it the power to conscript single women aged twenty to thirty and compel them to work in the armed services or industry. Married women without children could be directed to work within their locality. In 1944 the registration age for women was raised to fifty.

The majority of the female workforce in munitions manufacture had little prior experience of factory working. A survey taken in one South Wales ROF found that only five per cent of females had worked in a factory before. Ten per cent had never previously been employed and the rest had been employed as domestic servants, shop assistants, waitresses, dressmakers or clerical assistants.

For many young women who had worked in domestic service the alternative of working in a factory was appealing. The wages were attractive, too. One Bridgend girl earned £4 10s a week. Before working there she worked in a laundry and earned only 15s 11d per week.

Many parents, however, were reluctant for their daughters to work in the factories and this was a factor in slowing down recruitment in the early part of the war and there was some resentment in the mining communities at the level of wages being offered to young women compared to those in the mining industry. A miner's representative, interviewed by a Mass Observation researcher in 1942 told her:

> A man underground works like a slave. At the end of the week, he gets a matter of £3–15s. In some houses where the wife is an R.O. worker, she'll bring home £4–5. Then you have the psychological effect in the house.

During the mining apprentice boys strikes of May and June 1942 the Industrial Relations Officer for South Wales commented that 'the younger element were giving vent to the exasperation they feel when they find their sweethearts and sisters receive bigger wages than they do'.

The young women working in the munitions industry faced long working days. In both North and South Wales many travelled up to thirty miles there and back to work, spending up to three hours travelling to work on top of their shifts. Workers from Blaina, Monmouthshire, who travelled to the Glascoed munitions factory near Usk described their experiences to the Mass Observation researcher.

> Travelling's the snag. It gets people right down by the end of the week, especially the day shift workers. They have to catch the 4.10 a.m. train in the morning and get back here at 5p.m. in the evening.
>
> The buses they use should have been scrapped years ago, the windows are out and the floorboards are broken ... The travelling is a greater mental strain than the work itself.

The factories worked round the clock with three eight-hour shifts. Convoys of buses and trains left towns and villages transporting the women to work. Special munitions trains, as well as buses were used. For example, one left Swansea at 4am in the morning, heading for Bridgend.

Despite the stress and tedium of the travel the young women preferred the travelling to living in specially built hostel accommodation. In November 1941 only 2 per cent of hostels near Glascoed ROF were occupied whilst only 300 women had agreed to stay in the accommodation built in Bridgend to house up to 2,000. Some of the accommodation was later used to billet American soldiers and after they had left it was used to house prisoners of war.

For many of those that travelled it was a journey into danger, in more ways than one. The munitions factories were targets for enemy bombing. On the worst night of the war in North Wales, 31 August 1940, which saw the deaths of eleven people in the villages of Rhos and Penycae and much damage in the Wrexham area, the likely main target was the munitions factory at Marchwiel. Between June 1940 and July 1942 the Bridgend arsenal was a target on many occasions and whilst nearby villages such as Troes, Merthyr Mawr, Ewenny, Litchard and Laleston and parts of the town of Bridgend itself were hit, the munitions factory, remarkably, remained unscathed. The village of Rogerstone, north of Newport, where there was a factory making aeroplane parts, was attacked on numerous occasions and eleven people were killed and fifteen seriously injured in October 1941. Glascoed ROF came under direct enemy fire only twice. A worker was killed and several injured in one incident. The enemy plane was shot down and the pilot killed.

Miraculously then there were no major enemy hits on munitions factories that caused extensive death and injury, but tragically on 27 March 1944 nine workers on the night shift at the ROF in Llanishen, Cardiff, were killed by a stray shell fired from an anti-aircraft unit a mile away. Amongst those killed were a father and daughter who are remembered on the war memorial in the town of Caerphilly. The other casualties were all women workers.

The other dangers facing the workers were to do with the nature of the jobs that they were undertaking. Some women worked with TNT, which was a yellow powder and got into their skin and hair. It dyed their hair according to the colour – if they were blonde the hair went green, if they were black it went orange and if they were brunette it went yellow. Given that their skin was also discoloured yellow, they came to be known as the 'canaries'. In addition to the discolouration of skin there was also a high incidence of skin rashes and 'dust throats'. It is likely that many workers died prematurely due to TNT poisoning although there are no officially recorded cases. At the Royal Navy Propellant factory in Caerwent unusually high numbers of workers suffered from the early loss of teeth due to breathing of sulphur dioxide fumes. Here, workers left open the huge double doors that gave access to their working areas, even in winter, because working in the cold was preferable to the smell of gases.

Obviously the most deadly feature of TNT was that it was explosive. Working with live detonators there was a constant danger of an explosion. Many suffered from what might be termed 'ordinary' accidents in which workers split their fingers, were burned or lost a finger in a small blast. There were much more serious accidents in which people were killed or suffered horrible injuries. One worker, for example, lost her sight and both her hands in one accident. Exactly how many died is uncertain. It was officially forbidden to talk about any incidents outside of the factory. Mari Williams has identified at least twenty-two deaths from scouring local newspaper reports in South Wales. In more recent years specific events have come to light and have been recorded. Peter Phillips in his book *The German Great Escape* describes an accident in which three girls were killed on the Sunday afternoon shift at Bridgend on 18 May 1941.

In addition to working with the ever present threat of an explosion much of the work was tedious as the tasks undertaken were repetitive. A government select committee reported that the very nature of the jobs was a factor leading to low morale. Another factor was the tension in the relationships between managers and ordinary workers. A Mass Observation report 'People in Production' revealed this to be the case across industry in 1942 and the munitions factories are unlikely to have been an exception. Whilst there was an acknowledgement that there was a need to have stringent operation of safety regulations and security measures there were complaints that those who were responsible for carrying them out behaved as if they were sergeant majors or prison warders. The 'us' and 'them' ethos generated in wartime workplaces is a factor that may have influenced many workers to vote for the Labour Party in the first post-war General Election.

Whilst there were many causes for grievance in the factories there were those who found life there enjoyable. There was also a sense of camaraderie that could be likened to that of their male counterparts who worked in the collieries. The BBC radio programme 'Music While You Work' was played in the background to lighten the atmosphere. Many found companionship and friendship, which was more difficult to find in other working situations.

Despite grievances it should not be forgotten that the munitions factories made a vital contribution to the war effort. The work was carried out with remarkable efficiency, especially given the fact that it was done by a largely inexperienced workforce that had had to adapt to factory employment. In June 1944 the women at one munitions factory in Wales were singled out for praise by members of a House of Commons Select Committee on National Expenditure.

Shortly before the passing of the National Service Act, that introduced the conscription of women, the Ministry of Labour attempted a final campaign to recruit volunteers; 10,000 women were wanted from the six counties of North Wales 'to tip the scales against Hitler'. The campaign called for 5,000 to undertake work in munitions factories and another 5,000 to join the Auxiliary Territorial Services (ATS). The ATS had been created in 1938 with the aim of releasing men for combatant duties in the army. Members of the ATS became responsible for cooking, cleaning army quarters, looking after stores and equipment, undertaking clerical duties, driving and maintaining lighter lorries and vans, operating searchlights, signalling equipment and anti-aircraft (Ack-Ack) equipment. By December 1943 there were more than 200,000 members in the United Kingdom.

The North Wales recruitment campaign is interesting. It points out that there were dozens of different jobs that the ATS could do and that only one in ten would do cooking and orderly work. The ATS was by far the largest of the women's auxiliary services. The navy equivalent was the Women's Royal Naval Service (WRNS) and the air force equivalent the Women's Auxiliary Air Force (WAAF). Members of the WRNS were posted to a number of naval bases in Wales such as Holyhead and Milford Haven, and members of the WAAF were posted to the numerous airfields across Wales. As well as the traditional work of cooking, storekeeping, office work and driving they undertook more technical tasks such as wireless and radar operation and communication. Members of the WAAF became aircraft hands and were also engaged in packing parachutes. This was a complicated task which if done incorrectly could lead to the death of a pilot.

Alongside the appeals from the Ministry of Labour for women to work in munitions factories and to join the ATS there was a similar campaign from the Ministry of Agriculture to recruit for the Women's Land Army, whose members became more familiarly known as the Land Girls. By 1943 there were 87,000 in the UK with a sizeable percentage working in Wales. They undertook a wide range of tasks such as clearing and preparing land for crop growing, ploughing, harvesting, threshing, fencing, digging ditches, picking potatoes and other vegetables, cutting wood, sawing logs, driving tractors, livestock and poultry management, milking and milk delivery. One of the least popular jobs involved pest control, although a team of four girls operating in North Wales proved particularly adept. Travelling from farm to farm on their bicycles they managed to kill 35,545 rabbits, 7,869 rats, 1,668 foxes and 1,901 moles in just over one year.

A large number of the Land Girls worked in North Wales. There were 2,000 in Denbighshire. Many came from Lancashire where the textile mills appear to have been productive recruiting grounds. Many lived on the farms with the farmer's families but others lived in hostels. In Denbighshire, for example, there were hostels in Ruthin, Gresford, Overton, Wrexham and Abergele.

Living with the farmers and their families could be a hit and miss affair. One source claims that a billeting in rural Wales was not always a popular choice, stating that 'the Welsh farmer is usually more thrifty than the English and ... consequently his standard of living is less high.' One girl based on a lonely farm near Tregaron wrote to the WLA headquarters that her only entertainment was 'the weekly sermon in the village chapel where a hell-fire preacher denounced the evils of theatre going and whist drives'.

In South Wales there was a hostel at St Fagans, near Cardiff. Here the Land Girls worked at a tree nursery where they prepared the land for planting, planted seedlings and pruned growing trees. Later in the war they worked alongside German and Italian prisoners of war. Another hostel in South Wales was at Mount Ballon in Monmouthshire. The girls here produced a magazine called the *Mount Ballon Diary* which provides some first hand evidence of their experiences. The sixty-four girls organised their own social activities such as dances, concerts and cinema shows. There was a dramatic society and others attended needlework classes.

Not all the Land Girls worked on farms. Some volunteered for a special unit known as the Timber Corps. Centres were established in the Brechfa forest in Carmarthenshire, Milford Haven and Crickhowell. Some girls worked at a sawmill in Cardiff. The main purpose of the Timber Corps was to replace imported supplies of timber that could no longer be obtained. For example most of the pit props used in the South Wales coal industry had come from Portugal before the war. The girls felled trees and cut off and burned the branches.

Women worked in a wide range of other occupations which had previously been largely the preserve of men. The police established a Police Women's Auxiliary Corps. In Merthyr women were employed as telephonists. In Newport they were employed as drivers, clerical workers and canteen assistants. There was, however, resistance in some counties to employing women on the streets. The Chief Constable of Cardiff, for example, resisted throughout the war despite orders from the Home Office.

Women were employed as bus conductresses and on the railways, where some were involved in maintenance and others became station masters, as post office engineers helping to maintain the country's telephone and telegraph system and in shops where they took on specialist skills such as butchery that had usually been seen as a male occupation.

It should not be forgotten that women also continued to carry out work that had always been regarded as a women's occupation, and often found themselves in the front line as a result. The obvious examples of this were nurses. During the air raids on both Cardiff and Swansea, hospitals came under attack. As well as trying to ensure the safety of those patients who were already in their care, the nurses had also to receive and look after new casualties. Some nurses joined the 53rd Welsh General Hospital which assembled and trained at Llandeilo. They went to France to treat those soldiers wounded in the front line following the D-Day landings in June 1944.

Teachers also found themselves in the front line during air attacks and they had responsibility of leading the children in their care to shelters. Throughout the war teaching became predominantly a female profession as so many young male teachers were called up. However, it was not until 1944 that a regulation requiring female teachers to resign their post upon marriage was altered. The war years also saw the opening of day nurseries at which working mothers could leave their children whilst they were away at work. In Wales the move towards the opening of nurseries was slow. There were none in October 1941. Only when the Ministry of Health decided to pay a 100 per cent grant to local authorities to assist them with the costs of equipment and the building or adaptation of premises did they come into operation. A typical nursery at Trecenydd in Caerphilly was open from 9am to 5.30pm and catered for twenty-five children between the ages of two and five. There was a nominal charge of sixpence a day which included food. This example does, however, highlight a problem. The opening times did not entirely reflect the needs of women shift-workers, who were unable to take their children to nursery before leaving for work or collect them afterwards. There was still a need to rely on family, friends or neighbours for support.

Whilst the war saw a significant growth in the numbers of women in paid work it also saw the emergence of a major voluntary organisation, the Women's Voluntary Service for Civil Defence (WVS). Founded in

May 1938, it had 336,000 members by August 1939 and 1 million by 1941. Only 200 of these were paid. Its headquarters in Wales were in St Mary Street, Cardiff. An example of the acceleration in growth in the organisation is the Merthyr WVS. It first met on 19 September 1940 and by the end of the year it had 531 members. The activities of the WVS were many and varied but essentially their work revolved around air raid precautions, support for hospitals, support for the evacuation scheme, providing transport, raising funds for the war effort and leading salvage campaigns.

The minutes of the Merthyr group illustrate their heavy involvement with the evacuee scheme. On 22 November 1940 news was received that 1,000 children from Birmingham were due to arrive in the Borough. Next day it was reported that arrangements had been made for the children's reception at various schools and that beds had been prepared in case children had to sleep there in the event of insufficient billets having being found.

During air raids, volunteers acted as emergency ambulance drivers. There were 600 enrolled in the county of Glamorgan. After the air raids the WVS were there supporting those who had become homeless with the provision of emergency canteens. In March 1941 the three Cardiff-based WVS officers were commended for their efforts following the bombing raids on Swansea and Cardiff despite having to evacuate their offices. They had worked continuously, caring for those in shelters and feeding many air raid victims. Welsh-Americans provided twelve mobile canteens to the WVS in Wales. One of these came to Merthyr.

The contribution of women to the war effort is inestimable; however, similarly to the men who had found work during wartime after the Depression, there was a belief that employment would not continue after the war. A factory worker in Rogerstone told Mass Observation that 'The most general view is that there'll be a return to unemployment … that history will repeat itself, and I've the feeling that we shan't be wanted after the war.' Observations made in Blaina and Nantyglo suggest that people were already preparing for a post-war recession.

At least 50% of people are saving … trying to put a pound away for a rainy day … But the average British person is very shrewd and realises that there will probably be a slump. That's the reason why so many men and their wives are working now.

Mollie Tarrant – the Mass Observation researcher who conducted interviews in Blaina and Nantyglo – concluded that if the prophecies of a future slump materialised there would be a range of responses from women. Some would see the replacement of factory work with housework as 'a pleasant enough change' despite having to contend with a reduced income, whilst others would feel discontented.

In the immediate aftermath of the war thousands of female workers were demobilised and were replaced by men returning from the armed forces, and the old attitude that men should be the breadwinners and women should have responsibility for the home and family continued to hold sway. However, two significant things happened during the war that contributed to the changing role of women that took place during the second half of the twentieth century. Firstly, there was the beginning of the shift in the economy away from a dependence on heavy industry. Diversification of industry was to create more opportunities for women to work in the manufacturing sector. Secondly, the experiences of many women during wartime had increased confidence and raised expectations. Deidre Beddoe has written that

> Young women wanted a better, more affluent and more enjoyable life than their mothers before them: they wanted more than heavy domestic drudgery and successive pregnancies and they sought wider horizons than the four walls of their homes.

This new attitude was to be one of the driving forces for change in the succeeding decades.

## Chapter Five

# 1942–1944: Beveridge, Bevan and Discontent in the Coalfields

## The Beveridge Report

The two great turning points in the military history of the war against Nazi Germany were the victory in the North African desert at El Alamein in November 1942 and the German retreat from Stalingrad in January 1943. From this stage on, in the words of Angus Calder, 'the tide began to flow towards an allied victory'. It is a remarkable coincidence that at almost the midpoint between these two decisive events one of the most significant turning points in the domestic history of Britain occurred with the publication of the Beveridge Report on 1 December 1942.

Individual politicians had been agitating for the government to establish post-war aims for some time. Prominent amongst them was Aneurin Bevan, Labour MP for Ebbw Vale, and the newly-formed Commonwealth Party. At the end of 1942 there were emerging military circumstances that could justify a degree of focus on the end of the war, allied to a vehicle around which debate could be concentrated. Juliet Gardiner has written that, 'it really did seem in the New Year of 1943 that there would be a future to look forward to'.

The Beveridge report was ostensibly a review of existing social insurance schemes that had followed agitation by the TUC about the inadequacy of health insurance. The Cabinet set up the review in June 1941 and appointed Sir William Beveridge to become chairman. In reality it was much more; it was a vision of a post-war society free of want.

From the beginning Beveridge set his own agenda. Clearly the genesis of that agenda lay in the pre-war social conditions of poverty and unemployment. 'The purpose of victory,' he proclaimed 'is to live in a better world than the old world.' The report's proposals aimed to rationalise and unify the complex benefits system to ensure that all people had a basic minimum standard of living, especially at times when they could not earn. That is, when they were unemployed, when they suffered from sickness or injury and in their old age.

Henry Pelling has written that the most remarkable advances in social thinking embodied in the Beveridge Report are to be found in its initial 'assumptions', rather than its conclusions. Beveridge started off by taking it as accepted that the government would secure a high level of employment in the post-war world; that it would introduce family allowances; and that it would devise a comprehensive health service for all.

The Beveridge Report received popular acclamation, with nine out of ten people polled wanting its adoption. Beveridge proposed that his recommendations should be implemented from 1 July 1944, but the War Cabinet were of a different view, including some of the Labour Party members. Churchill in particular considered that it was a distraction from winning the war. They decided to accept sixteen of the twenty-three recommendations and proposed that work should begin on preparing legislation. Implementation, however, should be left to a new government, elected at the end of the war.

The National Council of Labour (the Labour Party and the TUC), endorsed the report and its implementation in line with Beveridge's proposal. Following the parliamentary debate on the government's response to the report, the ninety-seven members of the Labour Party who had no government responsibility voted against the advice of the War Cabinet and in support of early implementation. Altogether 119 MPs voted against the government, including David Lloyd George, making his last ever vote in the House of Commons. Angus Calder believes that the revolt by the Labour Party backbenchers did as much as anything to bring about a Labour Party victory in 1945, as the debate around the Beveridge Report came to symbolise the difference between Labour and Conservative in the eyes of the public.

The debate resonated throughout Wales. It revived memories of the Depression following the previous war and the need to ensure that it should not be repeated. The goal of full employment chimed with

1. Newspaper vendor, the day after war was declared. (*Western Mail*, 4 September 1939/by permission of Media Wales Ltd)

2. Royal Welsh Fusiliers leave Newtown for army camps near the coast just after the declaration of war in September 1939. (By permission of Llyfrgell Genedlaethol Cymru/The National Library of Wales)

3. Young evacuees from Birkenhead arrive at Newtown Station, September 1939. (By permission of Llyfrgell Genedlaethol Cymru/The National Library of Wales)

This Leaflet is published under the auspices of the Cwmparc "Bombed Area" Distress Fund Committee, and takes the form of an

# In Memoriam

Tribute to our Fellow-Villagers who fell victims to the murderous fury of Nazi war-planes on the night and morning of April 29/30th, 1941.

4. Evacuees at Usk. (*Western Mail*, 2 September 1939/ by permission of Media Wales Ltd)

5. Front page of memorial programme to commemorate the deaths of those who died in the bombing of Cwmparc in the Rhondda Valley. Three evacuee children and their mother were killed in the attack. (Courtesy of David Maddox)

6. Children in Montgomeryshire practising putting on their gasmasks in September 1939. In the early part of the war gas masks had to be carried at all times by everyone. (By permission of Llyfrgell Genedlaethol Cymru/The National Library of Wales)

7. Damage caused to a house by a bomb in Cwmparc. (By permission of the Glamorgan Record Office, South Wales Police archives)

8. A wider view of the damage caused by the bombing of Cwmparc. (By permission of the Glamorgan Record Office, South Wales Police archives)

9. Rescue workers with an unexploded bomb after a bombing raid near the Creigau Arms, Glamorgan. You can gain an idea of the size of bombs from this picture. (By permission of the Glamorgan Record Office, South Wales Police archives)

10. The inferno at the oil refinery at Pembroke Dock in August 1940. (By permission of the family of the late Vernon Scott, reporter for *The Western Telegraph*)

11. A German Junkers Ju88 shot down near Mallwyd in September 1940. (By permission of Llyfrgell Genedlaethol Cymru/The National Library of Wales)
*On 7 September 1940 the German Junker Ju88 was on a reconnaissance mission to the north-west of England. It was spotted and a Spitfire based at Hawarden attacked the plane and took out one of the engines. The Junkers Ju88, now with only one engine, was chased towards mid-Wales and the Spitfire attacked again. The German plane plunged to the ground on a mountainside near Mallwyd. All four airmen on board were badly injured and were taken to Machynlleth Hospital. They survived and were taken to a prisoner of war camp in Canada.* (From *No Landing Place* by Edward Doylerush)

12. The aftermath of a bombing raid near Barry. The remains of an Anderson Shelter can be seen in the foreground. (By permission of the Glamorgan Record Office, South Wales Police archives)

13. A purpose-built shelter provided for children at a school in Gresford, near Wrexham. They can be seen leaving the shelter after an air-raid exercise in 1939. (By permission of Llyfrgell Genedlaethol Cymru/The National Library of Wales)

14. Land reclamation between Machynlleth and Newtown in June 1941. In rural and mountainous areas reclamation was undertaken to increase the amount of land that could be used to grow crops and therefore reduce food shortages. (By permission of Llyfrgell Genedlaethol Cymru/The National Library of Wales)

15. Helping to win the war on the Kitchen Front. The Ministry of Food organised cookery classes and food demonstrations to show people how to improvise and use home-grown produce. This was a class in Newtown in October 1940. (By permission of Llyfrgell Genedlaethol Cymru/ The National Library of Wales)

16. A member of the Women's Land Army being given a tractor maintenance test in October 1943. Members had to pass practical and oral tests in a range of subjects, including dairying and dairy work, general farm work, hen breeding, tractor driving, horticulture, fruit production and pest control. (By permission of Llyfrgell Genedlaethol Cymru/The National Library of Wales)

17. David Lloyd George's last public appearance at Caernarvon in April 1940. (By permission of Llyfrgell Genedlaethol Cymru/The National Library of Wales) David Lloyd George had led the coalition government in the last years of the First World War. In May 1940 he made his last speech in the House of Commons supporting the call for Neville Chamberlain to resign and for a coalition government. In December 1942 he cast his last vote, supporting Labour Party rebels who wanted a commitment that the Beveridge Report recommendations would be introduced before the end of hostilities.

18. Aneurin Bevan's statue in Cardiff. (Courtesy of David Maddox) Bevan is primarily remembered as the founder of the National Health Service. His role as constant critic of the government during the Second World War is little known.

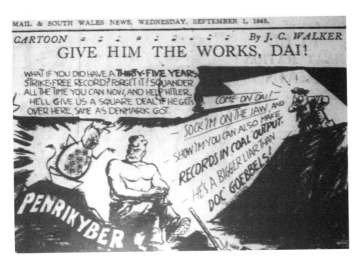

19. J.C. Walker Cartoon, *Western Mail*, 1 September 1943. (By permission of Media Wales Ltd) Created at the time of the Penrikyber Colliery dispute in September 1943, the cartoon presents an argument against the strikers.

# Britain's Treasures Were Buried in Wales

*The "Western Mail" suggests that an exhibition of the priceless pictures and works of art described below should be held in Wales before they are returned to their pre-war homes. The bringing together in Wales of so much treasure will probably never happen again.*

**From Our Own Correspondent**

ABERYSTWYTH, Friday.

IT may now be revealed that some of the nation's greatest treasures have been stored during the war in the National Library of Wales and in a tunnel burrowed into a hillside near-by.

Pictures, books, and ancient documents were brought there for safety in 1939. Never before, probably, has such a priceless collection been assembled in one place; their value cannot be translated into terms of money and their destruction would have been a loss to mankind.

In the tunnel, for instance, has been the famous Codex Sinaiticus, one of the earliest known texts of the Bible, which was found on Mount Sinai, and which was purchased for the British Museum for £100,000. Of interest to Wales are the Black Book of Carmarthen, the Bangor Pontifical, and the Howel Harris Diaries, all in excellent condition despite their five years underground.

**Other Treasures, Too**

FAMOUS paintings and other treasures have been stored in the Library itself, filling the spacious halls and overflowing to almost every nook and cranny in this lovely building. I am betraying no secret now by stating that the National Gallery found refuge here for many of its famous pictures during a very critical period of the war—from August, 1939, to September, 1941. Although they have gone, there are hundreds of masterpieces still at the Library, brought here by Government departments, Dulwich College and Boyman's Museum of Rotterdam, to mention only a few of the depositors. Incidentally, the Boyman's collection was brought here on its return from a New York exhibition.

Entrance to the tunnel.

20. The entrance to the cavern in Wales that stored precious art works throughout the war. The *Western Mail* story indicates that this information did not become public knowledge until the end of the war. (*Western Mail*, 5 May 1945/ by permission of Media Wales Ltd)

21. Celebrating the end of the war; a street party in Pembroke Dock. (Courtesy of Mrs Joan Watts)

people's hopes, as undoubtedly there was a fear that peace would lead to unemployment. There was also agreement on moving towards implementation as soon as possible to avoid the disillusionment of broken promises, as had happened at the end of the First World War. Added to war weariness, the government delay in responding to the report was a key factor in creating a mood of discontent, which was a feature of 1943, evidenced in South Wales by a wave of strikes in the mining industry.

In Wales, as elsewhere, the report brought discussion of the future to centre stage. One of the key actors on that stage was Aneurin Bevan, the man who was to be midwife to one of the three assumptions upon which the report was based – the introduction of a National Health Service.

## Aneurin Bevan

If there was one person whose name became synonymous with the Labour Government elected in July 1945, it was the Welsh firebrand, ardent reformer and architect of the National Health Service, the MP for Ebbw Vale, Aneurin Bevan. His elevation to a Cabinet post in July 1945 was all the more remarkable given his record during the war years as a radical, unafraid of voicing his views and convictions, whatever the circumstances. Throughout the war he was often to be an isolated critic of the coalition government and especially of the leadership of Winston Churchill. He often found himself amongst the twenty or thirty MPs that opposed government policies in Parliament. Yet, in December 1944 he was elected, in fifth place, on to the Labour Party's executive committee and seven months later found himself as a senior member of a new government, without ever having experienced government office at any level.

Bevan was a constant critic of government on matters of strategy for fighting the war. He opposed the existence of the Chamberlain government and then, when that was replaced by the Churchill led coalition, he opposed that on several crucial issues. He was a critic of the government on the domestic front, especially his Labour Party colleagues in the coalition, as he determined to continue to fight for social justice for the working class on issues such as the Means Test and workers' compensation. He was also determined that within the context of a war that was being fought in the defence of democracy that democratic principles should be constantly defended on the Home Front, hence the dispute that nearly led to his expulsion from the Labour Party in 1944.

Bevan may be perceived as an isolated figure in his various attacks on government throughout the war years but it must be remembered that there were other substantial indicators of widespread domestic discontent. Attitudes that may be interpreted by some as reflecting a quixotic individualism were actually representative of those held by many others. Bevan was far more in touch with swathes of public opinion than the majority of MPs. Within South Wales for example there was a significant degree of industrial unrest throughout 1942–1944, whilst in England a number of individuals who stood against coalition candidates in by-elections won remarkable victories. Tom Driberg standing as an independent socialist won a spectacular majority at Maldon in Essex in June 1942 and in April 1943 the newly formed Commonwealth Party that embraced the immediate introduction of the Beveridge Report won a stunning victory in rural Cheshire.

Within the press the *Daily Mirror* with its large working class readership was often perceived as an enemy of the Coalition and faced the possibility of prosecution in 1942. On the radio J.B. Priestly commanded large listening figures for his series of 'Postscripts' that provided a platform for his often anti-establishment views. He was eventually taken off the air. Bevan himself had his own mouthpiece in the press once he became editor of *Tribune*, the left wing weekly in 1942 and his performances in Parliament meant that his views became known in all newspapers, although they were criticised in most. The South Wales daily newspaper the *Western Mail* was a major critic.

Adept as he was with his pen, Bevan's great skill was as an orator. He used this talent to express his views to large crowds that came to listen to him, not only in the towns of his constituency, Ebbw Vale, Tredegar and Rhymney but right across South Wales. He spoke in workmen's halls and often in the open air such as at the Waun Pond site between Ebbw Vale and Tredegar where a memorial of standing stones has been erected to commemorate his achievements.

Bevan had nothing but vitriol for Neville Chamberlain. The outbreak of war in September 1939 was, to Bevan, the natural outcome of the policies that had been pursued by Chamberlain's government throughout the 1930s. The refusal to confront fascist aggressors had been a consistent theme as in the case of Mussolini's brutal takeover of Abyssinia, the failure to proffer any support to the Spanish Republican government against General Franco, and the appeasement of Hitler that had eventually led to the dismemberment of Czechoslovakia. At the same time there had been no effort to forge a closer relationship with the government of the Soviet Union, an attitude, which Bevan believed, had forced Stalin into making a pact with Hitler.

Throughout the period of the 'phoney war' Bevan attacked the government for not fully utilising resources in preparing for hostilities. Unemployment, which had fallen sharply in 1938 and early 1939, actually rose in the late months of 1939 and the early months of 1940. At the same time rationing was introduced. Bevan lamented the failure to grow more food at home whilst over a million were still unemployed.

His main focus of opposition was, however, Chamberlain. He maintained a constant hostility towards him and his close colleagues, the 'Men of Munich'. The 'very existence' of the Conservative government he said 'was worth armies to Hitler'.

On 4 April 1940 Chamberlain made a speech in which he defended his government's record since the outbreak of war. He stated that Hitler had failed to capitalise upon his initial superiority, 'our relative position towards the enemy has become a great deal stronger', Hitler had 'missed the bus'. This speech according to Bevan was yet further confirmation of Chamberlain's complacency. He responded by attacking the ranks of Conservative MPs whose support was keeping Chamberlain in office. They had been

… docile, sheep-like and uncritical of all the things done by those on the front-bench for the last two or three years. What are they waiting for? Are they waiting for some terrible calamity on sea or land or in the air before we can shake them out of this mood?'

Within a week Hitler had taken over Denmark and had landed troops in Norway.

One month later following a military disaster which led to British troops being evacuated from Trondheim in Norway, Parliament assembled to debate the conduct of the war. The debate was a major turning point in the history of the Second World War on the Home Front.

Chamberlain was forced to resign and Churchill took over as the Prime Minister of the coalition government that included the Labour Party. Thirty-three Conservative MPs had joined with the Labour Party in voting against Chamberlain and a further sixty abstained. Bevan was not called upon to speak in the debate, although one famous Welshman, making virtually the last major contribution of a long and vibrant political career, David Lloyd George, spoke strongly against Chamberlain.

Bevan was not entirely happy with the outcome of the debate. Chamberlain and other 'Men of Munich' still remained in government. There was not the clean break that he desired. Again, he found himself at variance with the leaders of his own party. He wanted them to be more aggressive within the Cabinet in pressing a distinctive point of view on domestic policy. He called upon them to press their colleagues in government for a more explicit expression of war aims beyond the defeat of Hitler. In the dark months following the evacuation from Dunkirk, the era of the Battle of Britain and the Blitz, he was arguing from a narrow base of support.

In late 1942, however, the publication of the Beveridge Report was to generate national debate about war aims on the Home Front. Bevan had been one of the few who had kept the debate alive in the intervening period, determined that a vision of working for a better society should not be lost despite the immediate requirement to defend the country. He criticised the Labour members of the coalition government for not having a bolder approach to social change, and for their tendency to perceive demands for war aims as a symptom of war weariness rather than a positive factor that could energise the nation.

Bevan was also concerned that in a war being fought to preserve democracy there should be a close adherence to democratic principles in practice. Measures to suppress freedom of speech, for example, should not be tolerated. He opposed the suppression of the *Daily Worker* and the threats made against the *Daily Mirror* when it published what the War Cabinet considered to be an inappropriate cartoon. On a civil liberties issue he came close to another expulsion from the Labour Party when he opposed legislation to make the incitement to strike illegal, which was hurriedly introduced following the unofficial coalfield stoppages in South Wales and Yorkshire in March and April 1944. He was particularly angry because the legislation was a response to Ernest Bevin's view that the strikes had been caused by a handful of Trotskyite agitators. This, Bevan believed, was an insult to the miners' intelligence and he accused the government of looking for scapegoats for the mess it had made of the mining industry. He upset Labour Party leaders because he was particularly vitriolic about full time union officials who had complied with the legislation.

Bevan avoided expulsion from the Labour Party by agreeing to sign an assurance that he would, in future, abide by the rules of the Parliamentary Labour Party. Michael Foot, Bevan's first biographer, believes that he agreed 'to swallow his pride' because of important work that needed to be done within the party.

> It is because I believe that there are elements in the Party which wish to continue association with the Tories when the war is over that I refuse to allow myself to be manoeuvred out of the Party and thus leave a clear field in which to accomplish the ruin of the Labour movement.

Three months later, in October 1944, Labour announced that it would fight the next general election as an independent party and in December Bevan was elected to its national executive, less than six months after moves had been made to expel him. He had played a critical role in ensuring that the war coalition remained just that, a coalition of necessity due to the exigencies of war.

## Industrial Discontent in the Mining Industry

In March 1944, the largest industrial stoppage in South Wales since the General Strike of 1926 took place. For nearly a fortnight almost 100,000 miners went on strike. It was unofficial and did not have the support of the miners' leaders. The timing appears to be remarkable. The miners had been foremost in urging the opening of the Second Front and it was well known that such a development was impending.

The *Western Mail*, the main South Wales daily newspaper, was particularly hostile to the strikers. In one editorial it claimed that the strike had begun 'without apparent cause and as though a malaise had suddenly descended on the valleys'. In another editorial it charged the strikers with

... wanton wickedness for which there is no extenuation ... nothing that Nazi propaganda had concocted to frustrate the Allies could do as much mischief as this dastardly attempt to hold the British people to ransom on the eve of invasion and in one of the greatest crises.

The *Western Mail* was being unduly provocative with its assertion that there was no apparent cause. The official historian of the wartime coal industry has claimed that the industry proved to be the most intractable of problems that the wartime government faced on the Home Front.

An alternative view put by the ILP newspaper the *New Leader* stated:

This strike was the result of pent-up feelings and bitterness of 25 years ... Even the government's behaviour towards the industry during the war, however, does not explain why the miners feel as they do today. It goes back long before 1939. It is all very well for the government to ask for the past to be forgotten, the miner cannot forget it, for it has left its scars too deeply.

This may be true, but it does not explain why the miners were acting in defiance of their elected leaders, why the strike was taking place at that particular time and the impact of wartime developments on the morale, mentality and strength of the workforce. The strike cannot be understood without an explanation of the wartime experience of the industry and its workers.

In July 1940 the TUC accepted the Condition of Employment and National Arbitration Order which amounted to the renunciation by the trade unions of the strike weapon. It became illegal for union officials to call their members out on strike. What it did not do, however, was to prevent rank and file workers organising unofficial strikes. Hence, the outstanding phenomenon of wartime industrial relations is the preponderance of unofficial strikes. Despite the fact that all strikes were unofficial, the years 1943 and 1944 saw more individual stoppages of work than any year since 1890. In 1943 1,800,000 working days were lost in 1,785 strikes and in 1944 2,194 strikes led to the loss of 3,700,000 working days.

In 1944 two-thirds of all strikes in Britain were in the coalmining industry. This was not an unusual statistic in terms of strike activity, given that during the period 1890–1945 there were more strikes in coalmining than in all other industries put together.

In South Wales there were 514 stoppages between the outbreak of the war and October 1944. The majority of these were short, averaging about three days, and were limited to one pit or district of a pit. A total of 3,777 pit days and 1,062,848 tons of coal were lost. Over half the days and over half the coal lost were in 1944, the year of the Porter Award strike. It lasted a fortnight and involved every pit in the coalfield except four.

The *Western Mail* claimed that the unofficial strikes affected the output of coal to a greater extent than the Allied bombing of the Ruhr affected German output, a claim clearly intended to have an emotive effect. On the other hand, David Grenfell, the Labour MP for Gower and Secretary of State for the Mines stated that time lost through strikes in the industry was less than one quarter of an hour per man per week and that the majority of men worked illegal overtime far in excess of that.

Whatever the merits or demerits of that particular argument it is difficult not to agree with the industrial economist Noah Barou, writing in 1947, that the unofficial strikes were testimony to 'unhealthy, unhappy and highly dangerous conditions in the industry'. Alan Bullock the biographer of Ernest Bevin, Minister of Labour during the war summed up the wartime mentality of the miners when he wrote:

> The miners are not lacking in patriotism, as their record in the fighting services shows, and there has never been any doubt about their strong political interest and of their hatred of Nazism. But in their attitudes to their own industry there was a conflict between the miners' undoubted patriotism and his strong sense of wrongs unremedied.

This attitude is probably best exemplified by miners from the upper part of the Swansea Valley who took part in the coalfield-wide stoppage of March 1944 and over twelve months earlier had participated in the making of a Ministry of Information film *The Silent Village*. In June 1942 a group of Czech partisans had assassinated Reinhard Heydrich. The assassination brought about fierce reprisals. All 173 adult males were taken from the mining village of Lidice and were massacred. The women and children were taken to concentration camps. It was an atrocity that resonated in the mining valleys of South Wales. Just three months after the massacre Humphrey Jennings, Director of the Ministry of Information Film Unit approached Arthur Horner, the SWMF President, and told him of his intention to make a film about Lidice. He was looking for a mining village which could reproduce the atmosphere and background of Czechoslovakia. Horner pointed him in the direction of Cwmgiedd at the top of the Swansea Valley and the local miners' agent Dai Dan Evans. Jennings held a meeting in the village at which he asked for the cooperation of the local community. Not only did he want the villagers to host his film crew, he wanted them to take part in the film which was to retell the story of Lidice as it could have happened if the Nazis had ruled in Wales.

The film unit lived in the miners' homes and spent four months working on the film. The people of the area played themselves and used their own names. The film opens with long shots of Cwmgiedd with the men making their way to work. In the local cinema children are shown enjoying a Donald Duck cartoon. The mood changes when loudspeakers announce a new 'Protectorate State' after the German invasion. Strikes are banned and the local miners' lodge is deemed to be no longer necessary. A small underground movement begins to develop with the production of an illegal Welsh language news-sheet. Pictures of guerrillas are shown in the woods and then the news is announced that the local Reich Protector, Heydrich, has been killed.

Following Heydrich's death Cwmgiedd is ordered to surrender the culprits by midnight. The villagers refuse to hand them over and at dawn the women and children are driven away in trucks. As the women are herded away they look down on their men folk standing against the church wall, facing the firing squad, defiantly singing 'Land of my Fathers'. The film ends with Dai Dan Evans delivering a eulogy to those who had died at Lidice.

There were no significant manifestations of discontent before 1942, although the issue of decline in coal output and manpower shortages had ensured that the coal industry was frequently in the press. Government intervention in the running of the industry and discussions on wages brought the industry to the centre stage during 1942. Apprentice boys' strikes, mainly in West Wales took place in June of that year.

For over two years the sense of common national danger had effectively dampened down the social conflict of the inter-war years. In 1942 the theatres of war moved away from Britain, and military events – the desert victory at El Alamein, the Battle of Midway that saw a major defeat for the Japanese and the lifting of the siege of Stalingrad – provided evidence at last that the fortunes of war were turning in favour of the Allies. The announcement of the Beveridge proposals for social insurance sparked debate about what was going to happen when peace came. At the same time war-weariness was becoming a factor, wartime restrictions were beginning to irritate and old grievances were beginning to resurface.

Wales had been a depressed area before the war and there were genuine fears that it would return to such a state afterwards. A Mass Observation investigation in 1942 reported that there was a 'prevalent feeling' amongst workers that after the war 'money will be tight and jobs scarce'. This was reflected in a local study carried out in Blaina and Nantyglo in which the central finding was that

> ... past communal experience shaped contemporary responses by miners and munitions workers towards wartime conditions and informed an outlook on the future ... There is a rising anxiety about the plight of the miner and his future prospects becoming more clearly manifest as the war situation improves.

Most people based their expectations on what had happened at the end of the First World War, and on this basis a victory for Britain could amount to a personal defeat for the employee.

Henry Pelling has written that one of the most remarkable features about wartime unrest was the almost entire absence of political motivation in the strikes that took place. K.G. Knowles – an academic who made a specialist study of strikes in the 1950s – agreed with Pelling.

> Unofficial strikes, in general, cannot be wholly ascribed to political poltergeists. One cannot agitate in a vacuum. Significantly, perhaps, the number of strikes reached its all-time maximum in the recent war, when Communist influence had been thrown into the opposite scale and the influence of the political splinters such as Trotskyists was more or less negligible.

In South Wales the Communist Party was relatively strong, and the miners union was led by a communist, Arthur Horner. In 1943 Communist Party members were actively supporting productivity drives and were urging the opening of a Second Front in Western Europe to relieve pressure on the Soviet forces fighting the Nazis.

In April 1944, however, Ernest Bevin did invoke a 'Red Scare'. He cited a Trotskyite group called the Revolutionary Communist Party. It had a national membership of about 250. They had come to prominence when four of their members were arrested and accused of inciting a strike in the North East of England shipyards against the Bevin Boy scheme designed to address the labour shortage in the mining industry – one in ten conscripts were to train as miners rather than join the armed forces. This was a fortnight after the end of the coalfield-wide Porter Award strike in South Wales.

The *Western Mail* on 8 April revealed that Trotskyites had been active during the coalfield strike:

> Their main activity during the strike was centred in a few pits, notably Merthyr Vale and Penallta. One of their leaders lives at Troedyrhiw, Merthyr and appears to have the support of some members of the Independent Labour Party.

The ILP was a left wing group that had opposed British participation in the war. It had three councillors in the Troedyrhiw area of Merthyr for most of the war years. Bevin's suggestion of a 'Red Scare' were vehemently attacked by Aneurin Bevan.

> It was an insult to the miners to suggest that they went on strike in opposition to their own leaders as a result of the advice and agitation of a small outside body of obscure political pedants. It was either an insult to the intelligence of the miners, or on the other hand to the public.

The wartime miner had many tangible grievances, some created by the war and others that had been present before hostilities. Sociologist Ferdinand Zweig maintains that the fact that the past weighed heavily on most miners' minds 'was the most important problem of the mines'. Nevertheless grievances created by wartime conditions cannot be ignored.

Wartime fatigue was a key factor. The average number of shifts worked by miners increased from five-and-a-half to five-and-three-quarters during the war. These shifts were being undertaken in deteriorating conditions by a workforce that was both ageing and inexperienced. By 1943 absenteeism rates were increasing but Angus Calder the author of *The People's War* has written in explanation that 'Absenteeism whatever adjective you gave it, was bound to increase as middle aged men who had suffered in many cases from years out of work, filled more shifts and contended with increasingly run down equipment.'

The increase in the average age of the workforce was a significant factor, and these men were working more shifts than before the war, with fewer holidays. This increase was created by the late decision of the government to make mining a reserved occupation. Over 20,000 miners left the industry between July 1939 and May 1941. It was the younger and stronger elements that left the industry whilst many of the men brought back into the industry were older and had not worked in the pits for some time. By 1944 the percentage of workmen employed under the age of forty-one was over ten per cent less (54.7) than it had been in 1939.

A memorandum from the Ministry of Fuel and Power to the War Cabinet in November 1943 considered that by that stage of the war, fatigue was having an impact on the best and most effective workers. The men were unaccustomed to such a long period of uninterrupted work and wartime conditions such as the blackout and rationing aggravated the problem.

During the war years there was a significant increase in the number of miners being certified with pneumoconiosis, the lung disease caused by coal dust, as medical opinion came to accept what miners had claimed for years, that coal dust was a killer. According to James Griffiths, MP for Llanelli, during each year of the war eighty-seven miners in South Wales died from the disease and a further 709 had become disabled. 'Perhaps people outside may realise better what that means when I say that every year we lose the equivalent of a pit in South Wales in this way.'

Working conditions deteriorated during the war. Many mines were old and were becoming increasingly difficult to work and the quality of materials was inferior. Bert Coombes described some of the timber that had to be used:

… before the war there were special sorts of timber for different jobs, but now the choice is restricted and rarely anything but oak arrives. This is tough, knotty stuff with an inside heart which rings like steel and often turns the sharp hatchet edge – causing a great deal of bad language. In the restricted spaces of the mine the extra hardness and weight of this timber is a definite hindrance and the miners will be glad to see the softer wood arriving again from abroad. Nor does oak bear the pressure well for it breaks without bending or warning.

As conditions worsened throughout the war, the accident rate increased. Between 1938 and 1942 the accident rate increased from 165 men per 1,000 to 239. The most serious accident in wartime Wales took place at the British Rhondda Colliery, Rhigos, when sixteen men and boys died. The *Aberdare Leader* put the accident into the context of the time.

> This column ... pays sorrowful tribute to the 16 colliers and collier boys who fighting the battle for more coal in Rhigos No. 4 drift lost their lives when an explosion ripped with terrible ferocity through the workings on Thursday night, July 10th 1941.
>
> The disaster in that level ... reminds us, now, when the British, Soviet and Allied people die from bomb blast for freedom from Nazi chains, that colliers and collier boys face perils in the bowels of the earth, and sometimes die, nearly every day, year after year, when there are no wars being fought.

As the war progressed, coal production fell. At the same time there was an increase in absenteeism which came under the spotlight in the press. Major Harry Llewellyn a former member of Montgomery's staff accused absentee miners of 'shooting our own fighting troops in the back' in a speech at the Rhigos Colliery. On the other hand, Trevor Evans the industrial correspondent of the *Daily Express,* a newspaper not usually sympathetic to the miners wrote,

> Generally men stay away because they are exhausted. Men are not machines. Do not think that I am excusing absenteeism. I merely seek to explain it.

Trevor Evans hailed from Merthyr.

Aneurin Bevan was typically combative in the miners defence – 'You could reduce absenteeism,' he said 'if the men had brass lungs, iron muscles and wooden heads'.

The younger members of the workforce were perhaps the most antagonistic towards their working conditions. They resented the fact that they did not have the opportunity to join the armed forces because they were tied to the industry by the Essential Works Order and the fact that their girlfriends working in munitions factories could be earning more than they was seen as a slight to their manhood.

There were two major outbreaks of boys' strikes – one in 1942 and one in October 1943. Their attitude was a cause of concern to the union leaders. James Griffiths, a miners' leader in West Wales and a minister in the post-war Labour government reminded his colleagues that these were

> … the children of the depression, reared on the dole, thrown on the scrapheap and allowed to rust. Their experience had bred distrust of anything with a suggestion of officialdom e.g. the union, the political parties, religious bodies etc.

The increase in restrictions due to wartime regulations began to irritate. There was an increase in prosecutions for offences such as persistent absenteeism, restriction of output and strikes. Some of the prosecutions were seen as being unnecessarily punitive and in some cases there was a perception that there was one law for the owners and another one for the miners.

There were three major disputes in 1943. One concerned a renewed flare-up of strike activity amongst the apprentice boys; the other two were in specific collieries and had their origin in industrial relations at colliery level. They raised the issues of inequality of sacrifice between workers and owners and fuelled the attitude that on the domestic front the end of the war would mean a return to low wages and unemployment.

In June 1943 twenty-four hauliers at Tarreni Colliery in the Swansea Valley were accused of deliberately restricting output. They were fined £20. Twenty men refused to pay and were sent to prison for a month. Soon eleven collieries in the vicinity of Tarreni were involved in sympathetic strike action. Tarreni Colliery had a history of poor industrial relations. In the period 1926–1939 there had been more stoppages there than any other colliery in the coalfield. For the first three years of the war the colliery had been strike free. Friction had begun in May 1942 which eventually led to the prosecutions just over a year later.

In late August 1943 there was a serious dispute at Penrikyber Colliery near Mountain Ash. This colliery had been strike free for thirty-five years.

The origins of the disagreement lay in a change of ownership of the colliery from Cory Brothers to Powell Duffryn. A change in management style was at the source of the dispute which was in danger of spreading to all forty-one collieries owned by the Powell Duffryn Company.

There was particular concern about this stoppage. Previous disputes had largely been in the western part of the coalfield in the mainly anthracite district where the pits were smaller scale. The steam coal area had been relatively strike free during the war.

The dispute at Penrikyber led to a special coalfield conference being called by the SWMF. According to Arthur Horner it was the most difficult meeting he had addressed in his seven years as president of the union. Every speech from the floor was an expression of discontent and extreme dissatisfaction. He described two incidents that were contributory to the mood. Both were from the Merthyr area. One was the fining of men at Lewis Merthyr Colliery for breaking blackout regulations and the other incident involved men from Merthyr who worked at Penallta Colliery near Ystrad Mynach. 130 men travelled the thirteen miles distance by bus. During a six-week period the men lost five shifts due to the lateness of the bus. They were not allowed down the colliery. On 8 June 1943 the bus was so late leaving Merthyr that many refused to get on, aware that in previous weeks they had not been allowed down. These men were sued for breach of contract and were fined in the County Court. These two examples may seem trivial but they helped to create what Horner described as 'inflammable human material'.

The erosion of customs was the cause of some strikes, including the coalfield stoppage of March 1944 when allowances for housecoal, working in water and contributions to the cost of tools were incorporated into the newly proposed minimum wage. This aroused criticism from the press and some union officials. One SWMF official told his members 'they shouldn't expect to cling on their old traditions and customs when their comrades in other lands were working as slaves.' Bert Coombes, in his documentary novel *Miners Day* responded to this charge:

> I want to assert that most customs in the mine have a background reason. When the papers tell you so sarcastically that a thousand men are on strike because of what happened to one, try to believe that each of those thousand men have a mind and some responsibilities ... It is very often

the case that the miners feel that they must retain some customs and privileges for those brothers and friends who are away fighting, and will some day have to come back to the mining industry.

In August 1943 Arthur Horner warned the coalowners that

... there is a growth of feeling that the home war is becoming more important than the other war. With the departure of the fear of invasion of this country there are people beginning to believe that it is more important to set about preparing ramparts for the struggle at home after the war than to see the war through.

One factor causing strikes was the issue of wages. Miners entered the war with a sense of grievance over pay. The issue was exacerbated in the early years when discontent over the basic wage was aggravated by the knowledge that men who worked in the munitions factories earned higher wages. Professor Court, who wrote the official history of the coal industry after the war, can be quoted here. 'The comparisons between what a man could earn in the pit, after years of experience, with what others could earn in the Royal Ordnance factories, with hardly any training at all, was of the sort that struck home to the dullest.'

The complaint of the miners was not that the wages were too high in the munitions factories, but that wages in mining had ceased to bear any relation to the skill and exertion required, even to the standards established in other industries. The introduction of the EWO added insult to injury because a miner could not leave his industry to go and work in a munitions factory. After May 1941 there were quite a large group of miners who had been transferred back into mining from factories. It is estimated that transfer may have cost them between £1 and £2.50 a week (the minimum wage was approximately £4.30 after 1942).

A new minimum wage of £4 3s was awarded in June 1942. For the first time since the war began the miners had a real increase relative to the cost of living. Aneurin Bevan, however, thought that the increases were inadequate and that the rewards in mining were still well below those in other trades. Alan Bullock the biographer of Ernest Bevin wrote:

For more than a century Britain's industrial strength had rested on the foundation of a cheap and abundant supply of coal. In the 1940s it was belatedly forced to recognise that if it had been cheap in money costs, it had been purchased at too high a price of human misery, suffering and resentment. Neither Bevin nor anyone else could remove within a year or two the social and psychological consequences of the long and bitter history of the mining industry.

He was writing in retrospect, of course, aware that eighteen months later there was to be a coalfield stoppage in South Wales, followed by one in Yorkshire.

In October 1943 the MFGB put in a claim for a minimum wage of £6 a week. A week afterwards there was a two-day debate in the House of Commons to discuss the mining industry – output was still falling, there was still a manpower shortage and industrial relations were deteriorating. A wages campaign was undertaken by the miners union and the Porter Tribunal was established to investigate and pronounce on the claim.

The issue of nationalisation was raised. Churchill expressed the maxim that the guiding principle of the coalition government should be 'everything for the war, whether controversial or not, and nothing controversial that is not *bona fide* for the war'. Nationalisation of the mines, he maintained, was not a necessary step to be taken towards the winning of the war. Professor Court considers Churchill's intervention to be one of the most successful efforts of throwing oil upon troubled waters that Parliament saw that year. Bevan felt that it was a significant underlying cause of the crisis that erupted in the coalfields in March 1944.

There was increasing tension in the industry in the last months of 1943 and relationships between colliery management and miners were clearly deteriorating at local level. A special coalfield conference was called for the 3 January 1944; Horner spoke as follows:

We are now in the third day of the year and already there are two strikes in big pits in the coalfield. This is clear indication that something is radically wrong in the mood of the coalfield at present. There is a feeling that the war is already won and now is the time for workers to redress long standing wrongs they have endured for years. In fact, the next few months will be the most momentous in the history of the war. Thousands upon thousands are due to die in the great onslaught that is to be made on the continent of Europe.

The SWMF circulated a statement to all its members which said that it was deeply conscious of the great wrongs that miners had suffered in the twenty years before the war but called upon them to cease all unofficial strikes and put the maximum of effort into the struggle against fascism.

The Porter Award was announced on 23 January. The minimum wage was to be £1 less than the miners' claim and many allowances for special circumstances were now incorporated into the minimum wage. The SWMF immediately issued a statement condemning the award but saying that issues raised should be dealt with constitutionally. This lead was generally followed.

Three weeks later the government announced that anomalies could be discussed and funded at local level. The coalowners responded by stating that the award should be paid for by the government. The discussions dragged on and seemingly out of impatience the strike erupted on Monday 6 March. It started in Monmouthshire and by Thursday virtually the whole coalfield was on strike. By the end of the following week there had been a general drift back to work.

The *South Wales Evening Post* told the miners that they were throwing away 'very real public sympathy and understanding that had been built up during the war'. This was the view supported by Professor Court who felt that the public were irritated at the distraction from impending military events.

Within the mining communities traditional loyalties held fast. Bert Coombes countered the charge that the miners were betraying the armed forces. When his colliery discussed strike action the argument that to strike would let the soldiers down was the main bone of contention. It was countered by those who had brothers and sons in the forces who urged them to fight for them so that they would have something to return to when they came home. Coombes wrote at the end of the strike:

> Possibly our actions were wrong in view of the circumstances, but it was the climax to a series of happenings that should have been avoided. It was an outlet of a seething disgust for the continual delays and evasions, intensified by the feeling that men who knew nothing of our work or our ideas were making decisions that would affect our lives and families. On going back to work we felt we had made our protest and there was a relief in returning.

On 12 April following a further coalfield-wide strike in Yorkshire the government agreed to fund the anomalies with £1,750,000.

The Porter Award strike brought to an end twelve months of particular restlessness and turbulence in the coalfield, however, it did not quell underlying feelings. Will Lawther, President of the Miners Federation of Great Britain wrote:

> A point has been reached where I frankly declare that the miners are in a mood of sullen resentment and anger in relation to their own industry, a mood so deep that no matter what proposals are made in regard to wages and working conditions, their confidence in the industry will never be restored until it has been taken over by the state.

There was however a significant response on the output front following the Normandy Landings. In the week after the invasion the *Aberdare Leader* reported that four pits in the valley had broken their output targets and the others reported a substantial improvement. In the closing months of the war the leadership of the union began to re-assert its control and directed energies towards the election of a Labour government with an agenda for the nationalisation of the industry.

## Chapter Six

# Incomers – Bevin Boys, Yanks and Prisoners of War

## Bevin Boys

Between January 1944 and March 1945, 4,783 young men trained to become miners in the South Wales coalfield as a result of conscription. They were part of the government's solution to one of the most intractable problems that it faced on the Home Front – the fall in coal output. Some of these young men came from parts of Wales, but others came from England. They came from all sorts of backgrounds a long way from coalfield towns and villages. Many were middle class and had trained for white-collar work in shops and offices. Many had begun to prepare themselves for military life by joining the army or air force cadets and had set their heart on joining the armed services. All that most had in common was the fact that the last digit of their call-up registration number was the same and that it had been chosen as the means of selecting which new conscripts entered the armed services and which ones would be directed to work in the mines, in the fortnightly ballots that took place after 14 December 1943.

These young men became known as the 'Bevin Boys' after Ernest Bevin, the Minister for Labour, whose department was responsible for the scheme. Many took up the challenge with reluctance. Of the 21,800 who eventually became a part of the scheme across Britain, 40 per cent appealed against the decision but very few were successful; 500 were prosecuted for refusing to take part and 197 were sent to prison, although they would quite willingly have fought in the armed forces. On Tyneside and around Huddersfield there were large protest strikes following the conscription of apprentices. In South Wales this strike extended to the shipyards at Barry when thirty-eight apprentice ship repairers protested against one of their members being drafted into coalmining employment.

The Bevin Boys arrived at the collieries at a time when morale in the coalmining workforce was extremely low. The manpower shortage had been highlighted in May 1941 when it became clear that the industry was incapable of meeting the output demands. At this time the call-up of miners into the armed forces was stopped. Although calls were made for the release of skilled colliers from the forces, these were dismissed as being disruptive and impractical. Appeals to other ex-coalminers who were working in industry proved unsuccessful. Many of those that did return were surface men whilst the priority need was for underground workers. In September 1942 it was decided that all young men under the age of twenty-five who were eligible for military service should be given the option of volunteering for work in coalmines. Despite all attempts to promote opting for work in the mines as a patriotic act, very few made the choice and just over twelve months later it was decided to introduce a compulsory scheme.

By 1943 the manpower in all industries was beginning to suffer from war weariness and fatigue. There were, however, additional stresses facing workers in the mining industry. The manpower shortage had been evident from very early stages of the war, but the exodus of the younger and stronger elements in the period before May 1941 had had a long-term impact. By 1944 the average age of a miner in South Wales had increased significantly. This ageing workforce was more susceptible to illness and particularly fatigue. In a memorandum to the Cabinet in November 1943 the Ministry of Fuel and Power considered that war fatigue was having an effect on the best and most effective workers. A long period of uninterrupted work in wartime conditions such as the blackout and rationing aggravated the problem. Although the older miners were the steadiest workers they were finding the going hard. Furthermore, there was a widespread view that workers had entered the war with a lower standard of health than had been the case in the previous war due to the harsh Depression years.

In South Wales there was an additional medical problem that became much higher profile in July 1943 when it was legally recognised that coal dust was a killer. It became possible for miners who suffered from pneumoconiosis – caused by coal dust in the lungs congealing into a cemented mass – to apply for compensation. It became clear in the following years that many sick men had been toiling in their workplaces whilst suffering from the disease.

The mood amongst workers in the industry at the end of 1943 was sullen and resentful. The output crisis had placed the industry under a continuous spotlight in the press and there was a sense of injustice at the criticisms of some newspapers. When the Bevin Boy scheme was introduced there was widespread cynicism about its purpose and potential effectiveness. The SWMF considered it to be totally beyond the capacity of the manpower of the industry to produce anything like the quantities of coal required and were insistent that only the recall of men from the armed forces would be effective. The appearance of hundreds of trainees with no background in the industry was seen by many as another unnecessary burden. A correspondent to the *Aberdare Leader* suggested that it was more likely that production would be reduced, as the Coal Mines Act demanded that an inexperienced worker at the coalface must be under the care of an experienced one. The responsibility for teaching and safeguarding his inexperienced mate would most likely handicap the output of the experienced miner.

In South Wales a training centre was opened at Oakdale Colliery in Monmouthshire. A purpose-built hostel was also erected at Oakdale to house the trainees during the initial training period. Other hostels were built in Aberdare, Bryncethin, Pontypridd and Ystrad Mynach for use once the trainees were attached to collieries. Trainees allocated to work in the North Wales coalfield went to Swinton in Lancashire for their initiation.

The first trainees arrived at Oakdale on 18 January 1944. The initial training programme was four weeks long. There were four elements to the programme. A quarter of the time was spent following a physical training schedule directed by men who had worked on armed services programmes. This element of training was in recognition that there was a need to be physically fit to undertake work in the mines.

A further quarter of the programme was classroom-based with trainees learning about health and safety procedures and other technical aspects of mining. The rest of the programme was at the colliery learning about surface work and underground tasks.

After the first phase of training the Bevin Boys went to their allotted place of work where they undertook tasks on the surface for the first four weeks and then spent another four weeks underground under the supervision of an experienced miner. They had to spend four months working underground before working at the coalface.

There was little evidence that the scheme had any impact on improving output. A small percentage actually went on to work at the coal-face and the majority were engaged in underground work, ancillary to actual coal-getting, for example, maintenance of haulage roads, attaching and detaching coal tubs and trams. By doing these tasks, however, it released other men to be upgraded for work as coal-getters.

The absenteeism record of the Bevin Boys was said to be half as much again as that for other miners. It is also probable, that the accident rate for these newcomers to heavy industry was higher, too.

The Bevin Boys initially stayed in the hostel closest to their training centre. These were Nissan huts in which there were twelve beds and lockers. There was also a shower block and a recreational block with a dining room, lounge and games room. Once allotted a place of work they could either go to another of the purpose-built hostels or to a private billet. Harvey Alford, a Bevin Boy working in Ogmore Vale was advised by miners there to try and find private lodgings as he would be better off if he could get in with a good family. He was lucky in finding 'a second mother'.

The majority of Bevin Boys were well received but often had to overcome initial suspicions. There was a misapprehension amongst some people that they were conscientious objectors. It was also difficult to be complete outsiders in what could be quite closed communities. One Bevin Boy has described how few people spoke to him in the first six weeks of his time at a colliery. However once the 'ice' was broken he got on well with his workmates. Only at one colliery – Elliot's in New Tredegar – did colliers refuse to work with the Bevin Boys, but this dispute was soon resolved.

Life was hard for the Bevin Boys both at work and socially. Large numbers would have preferred to have given their war effort in one of the armed services. Their working conditions were gruelling and physically demanding. They arrived in the industry at a very difficult time when miners were feeling undervalued and perceived the young men as burdens. Arthur Horner, the president of the South Wales miners, passing his verdict on the scheme in April 1945 claimed that it had been nonsense to expect that trainees sent to the mines for the first time could have compensated for the loss of skilled miners. However, whilst their impact in terms of boosting production was negligible, once they returned home many became great advocates for the miners' cause. They were able to bring home to the public what the job was like and why it was so unpopular. A conscript from Barnes in Surrey has written that:

> It was an eye-opener to my family ... They came to understand a lot more about the miners' life, especially after my lifelong friend was killed in a shaft only six months after joining ... We could all understand the attitude of the miners against the mine owners. They didn't strike me as militant. They weren't an aggressive, rabid people.

In the circumstances the majority coped well and made the best of the situation that they were in. Recognition, however, was belated. Although they had arrived in their places of work as a result of conscription they did not receive 'civvie' clothing on finishing their time, as soldiers, sailors and airmen did, and no medals were given for their service. Only as late as 1998 has there been public acknowledgement of their role. Since then they have been represented at the annual Remembrance Day ceremony at the Cenotaph in Whitehall.

## Yanks

The Japanese attack on Pearl Harbour was a major turning point of the Second World War, the ripples from which were to have a heavy impact on the role of Valley airfield on Anglesey and the Bristol Channel ports of South Wales. Life in the homes of particular families was to change, new excitement was brought into the lives of youngsters in some communities and the lives of some young women were to be set in a completely unexpected direction.

By the time of D-Day, June 1944, there were approximately 1,500,000 American combat and service troops in Britain. Over 50 per cent arrived between January 1944 and D-Day. These were mainly ground forces who had undertaken their initial training on the other side of the Atlantic. Until August 1943 the majority had been service staff and airmen, although some soldiers had come over and been involved in the campaigns in North Africa and Italy. South Wales, from Newport in the east to Pembroke in the west became host to approximately 100,000 Americans.

The period of American activity in Wales has been described as an interlude in history. This description is appropriate in two contexts. For RAF Valley and the ports of South Wales it was a time of unprecedented activity. Seventy-eight per cent of supplies for the American forces passed through the docks of South Wales which handled six times as much traffic as they had done pre-war. Penarth has been described as being 'virtually an American town in the year before D-Day'. Huge quantities of food came into Barry Docks to feed the Americans based in the region of south-west England and South Wales. At Dunraven Park, Southerndown, the Americans had their own bakery that used white flour, unavailable in ration bound Britain, and they roasted and ground imported coffee beans. The bread and coffee were distributed across the area from Cornwall to Pembroke. In some cases various communities were almost taken over for a short time.

The time in South Wales was an interlude for the Americans themselves. Many came to South Wales for just a few months, a time in between training for combat and the combat itself. For young men about to go into military action, it was the lull before the storm. They may be remembered for their music, their dances, their carefree morality, their brashness and their relative affluence, but for many, this period was a prelude to death or injury on the battlefield. The 28th Infantry Battalion, based at Island Farm, Bridgend and Porthcawl, lost over 75 per cent of its men during the campaign after D-Day, the heaviest losses of all American divisions.

Whilst death on the front line in Europe awaited many, unfortunately the hills of Wales were to prove both inhospitable and deadly for over 130 members of the US Air Force, the USAAF. A series of plaques on remote mountain tops and other crash sites remain as testimony to these fatalities. Wales for these young servicemen was an unknown land that became their final resting place.

Initially it was the American participation in the air war against Germany that had been the greatest priority. East Anglia became a patchwork quilt of airfields. The changing nature of the air war led to the transformation in the role of RAF Valley from the summer of 1943. As enemy activity over

North Wales diminished there was less of a need to provide fighter cover for the region. At the same time, however, the Americans were arriving in Britain in increasing numbers in preparation for the invasion of mainland Europe. Prestwick in Scotland was the transatlantic terminal for fighter aircraft from the US. A second base was needed, both to supplement Prestwick and as a bad weather alternative.

Valley was chosen because of its location on the west coast and its proximity to the US depots at Burtonwood and Warton in Lancashire. From July 1943 the RAF units there began to take second place to the Americans. Heavy bombers arrived on almost a daily basis. Following long and often dangerous flights they would have a brief stay at Valley and then take off for their final destinations, which were usually air-fields in East Anglia from where they launched their bombing offensives against Germany, occupied France and Vichy France. The influx of bombers continued until May 1945, when the war against Germany ended. Almost immediately the role of Valley reversed, as between June and August 1945 some 2,500 aircraft and their crews returned home to the US. The scale of activity at its peak was phenomenal. Each month up to 500 aircraft arrived and approximately 4,000 men had to be received, processed, fed, billeted and sent on to operational units.

The safety record at Valley was extremely good and there were no crashes on the airfield itself, but a number of flights en route to Valley suffered horrendous accidents. One particularly tragic case occurred on the night of 22 December 1944 and involved a bomber that was based at Cheddington in Buckinghamshire. It was one of a group of seven involved in a mission during the Battle of the Ardennes. On returning to England bad weather forced them to divert to the Kent coast where they landed safely. When they next attempted to reach Cheddington, they were diverted again to Atcham, near Shrewsbury. This airfield, too, was in the grip of bad weather, and although four planes landed the other three were diverted yet again, this time to Valley. By the time they reached Valley, they were low on fuel, there was heavy cloud and there were three other planes waiting to land. The B24, serial number 42-51232 was also having problems with its radio. With the fuel shortage becoming desperate, the pilot instructed eight members of his crew to bail out. Unknown to him the plane was on the seaward side of the airfield. None of the men, destined for the icy water, was wearing a life jacket. Despite the efforts of the Holyhead Lifeboat no bodies were found. The pilot and the co-pilot bailed out shortly afterwards and both found the safety of dry land. The plane crashed into the sea near to North Stack cliffs. The other two bombers landed safely.

Even greater loss of life occurred on 8 June 1945, shortly after the war with Germany was over and the Americans were returning home. On this day a Boeing B-17G Fortress with twenty airmen on board was on the first leg of its journey from the Polebrook airbase in Northamptonshire. The plan was to stopover at Valley for refuelling. They reached the North Wales coast near Barmouth. The cloud cover was heavy when the pilot requested a course for Valley. On turning right towards the airfield he crashed the plane into the side of Craig Cwm Llwyd at 1,100 feet, whereupon it careered another 300 feet, burst into flames and exploded. There were no survivors. It is unclear as to the exact cause of this navigational error, but one theory suggested is that magnetic ores in the mountain may have affected the planes compass. A memorial has been erected on the site of the crash.

The Craig Cwm Llwyd accident had the highest death toll of any single air crash during the war years in Wales. On the night of 16 September 1943, however, another twenty American airmen died as a result of two separate incidents. The planes that crashed were a part of USAAF bomb squadrons stationed in Norfolk. They had been detailed to attack the airfield and a bomb factory at Bordeaux in south-west France. When the target area was reached the mission had to be abandoned because of heavy cloud. The opportunity was taken to bomb targets at La Rochelle. Here they came under heavy fire themselves. On arriving back off the coast of Cornwall they encountered heavy rain. As darkness descended each member of the group endeavoured to make its way back to base individually. Boeing B-17F Fortress 42-5903, also known as *Ascend Charlie*, had had one of its engines hit during the raid on La Rochelle. It was last reported seen by other members of its squadron approaching the English coast at 20.17 hours. Just over an hour later it crashed on top of Pen Gwyllt Meirch in the Black Mountains, north-west of Abergavenny, killing all ten on board. To the west a similar fate befell Boeing B-17 Fortress 42-5906, also known as *Sondra Kay*. The plane flew into Rhiw Gwraidd at Upper Cilgee near Rhayader. The entire crew of ten were killed.

These four incidents alone accounted for forty-eight deaths. Due to the work of Edward Doylerush and Roy Sloan who have written about air accidents in Wales it is possible to compile a record of other accidents that led to the loss of American life. This sad litany can be found below.

**11 August 1942** – Boeing B-17E Fortress 41-9098. The crew of this aircraft, based at Polebrook, were on a training exercise when they crashed into Cadair Bronwen in the Berwyn Mountains. All eleven on board were killed.

**23 August 1942** – Douglas C-47 Skytrain, 41-7803, a transport plane. The plane was on the last leg of a journey from Connecticut to the US base at Atcham near Shrewsbury, via Labrador, Greenland, Iceland and Prestwick in Scotland. It was carrying twelve men and supplies from Prestwick to Atcham. In thick mist it crashed into the summit of Moel-y-Gaer in the Llantysilio Mountains north-west of Llangollen. Eleven of the men on board were killed. The survivor, air mechanic George Lesikar was led to safety by a local shepherd and taken to Wrexham hospital.

**4 August 1943** – Boeing B-17F Fortress 42-3124. The bomber was on a navigational training exercise from USAAF Molesworth. It flew into the western side of Arenwig Fawr at 2,800 feet. All eight personnel on board were killed. A plaque to their memory has been placed on the side of the Old Town Hall in Bala.

**29 December 1943** – Boeing B-17F Fortress 42-5791. The aircraft, from Horham in Suffolk ferrying airmen to Southport, crashed into Cwm Mountain in the Clwydian range. Visibility was poor. The eighteen crew and passengers all died.

**7 January 1944** – B24J Liberator 42-99991. *Bachelor's Baby* as the plane was known had flown into RAF Valley on 3 January after the long haul from the US. The weather was bad with low cloud, fog patches and intermittent rain. There were eleven men on board. The pilot recognised that he was in trouble, flying at a dangerously low height approaching the coastal village of Llanfairfechan. He clipped the roof of a house, took the tops off a line of trees and eventually ploughed into the foot of Moelfre Mountain. Three of the passengers were killed and two later died from their injuries.

**24 August 1944** – Liberator PB4Y1 38753. This US Navy plane, based in Devon, was on a night flying training exercise when it crashed on high ground near Brecon, killing the six men on board.

**12 November 1944** – Douglas c-47B Skytrain 43-48473. This transport plane, with a crew of four, was carrying a cargo of mail and freight from the newly liberated Le Bourget airport in Paris to the American base at Burtonwood near Warrington. Due to fog in Lancashire the plane was diverted to Valley. It never made it, having flown into the top of cliffs above Llyn Dulyn. It was ten days before the wreck was found. There were no survivors.

**1 February 1945** – Martin B26G Marauder 44-68072. A medium-sized bomber with a crew of five. It had flown from Florida to Brazil, to Dakar in West Africa, to Marrakesh in Morocco and on to St Mawgan in Cornwall. Its final destination was due to be Burtonwood. It struck the summit of Y Garn above the Llanberis Pass. All the crew were killed. A plaque in their memory has been placed in a layby in the Pass.

**18 March 1945** – B24 Liberator 42-95036. It was on a training flight from its base at Harrington, Northamptonshire, when it hit a rising slope on Disgynfa above the village of Llangynog in the Berwyn Mountains. It bounced on to the top of the mountain and the nose section was smashed. Four members of the crew were killed and five were rescued.

In addition to these accidents in which there were multiple deaths there were at least eleven other incidents in which US fighter pilots, usually on training exercises, were killed. The mountains of Wales, so often a protection against invaders in the past, proved to be fatal to some American allies.

Apart from at Valley there were few members of the US Air Force based in Wales. The main locus of operations for the Americans was in the ports along the coast of South Wales making preparations for the invasion of Europe. The first Americans that came to South Wales landed in Newport and were located at camps in Malpas and Tredegar Park. In Cardiff and the surrounding area there were a number of camps. These were either newly constructed or existing British Army barracks. At Island Farm, Bridgend, accommodation that had originally been built for female munitions workers was utilised and in Caerphilly a complex built to house people who might have lost their homes through German bombing was adapted. The American camps have been described as 'a self-contained slice of the USA'. Both Island Farm and the Caerphilly camp were later to be used to house German prisoners of war.

The work of two local historians, Bryan Morse, author of *A Moment in History – The Story of the American Army in the Rhondda in 1944*, and Dennis G. Sellwood who wrote *The Friendly Invasion*, an account of American soldiers who passed through Caerphilly in 1943–1944, have provided an invaluable service in recalling this episode in history using their own research and accounts of local people and surviving American servicemen.

According to Bryan Morse, 3 per cent of Americans were billeted in private homes. It would appear that this experience was therefore a quite specific one for the people of Pontypridd, the Rhondda Valleys and Caerphilly. Over 3,000 Americans were billeted in the Rhondda and Pontypridd and approximately 280 in Caerphilly. The responsibility for the billeting was in the hands of the local police forces. Some billeting was voluntary but in some cases there was compulsion. The police knew which houses had spare rooms and the Americans provided metal frame beds if they were required. The billeting was for sleeping purposes only; food was taken in the army mess. Special arrangements had to be made for the purposes of showering. In Pontypridd a local colliery which had pithead baths was utilised whilst at Porth the local swimming pool was used. The exercise proved to be remarkably successful; the young men were welcomed wholeheartedly into the majority of homes. There were some cases where the arrangement did not work out, but these seem to have been relatively rare.

The Americans who came to Caerphilly were in the service side of the military operation. Charles Art Ryan, who was with the 634th Quartermaster (Laundry) Company based in Caerphilly, provided a lot of information to Dennis Sellwood. This is what he wrote about the vital role of the support services.

I think it is important to realise that it takes around ten soldiers to do back-up services for a single frontline soldier. This includes vehicle drivers, cooks, laundry companies, shower units, weapon repair units, shoe repair units, food depots, arsenals, heavy to light ordnance repair units motor pools etc …

The other soldiers based in Caerphilly belonged to two railway battalions. They worked in the railway workshops at Newport, ensuring that the huge 100-ton locomotives that had been transported across the Atlantic into Britain in readiness for use in France following the invasion were in good working order before further transportation. This was a massive operation. Part of the old Barry railway was closed and given up for storage. For over a mile-and-a-half from Tonteg to Treforest there was a line of 119 huge locomotives one after another. A further 152 were stored in Penrhos sidings near Caerphilly, over 60 were in sidings at Llanbradach and another 84 at Cadoxton, near Barry. Once the locomotives were overhauled the engineers had to go to the various docks to fit the ships to enable them to transport the locomotives.

The soldiers billeted in the Rhondda were primarily stevedores. They had been working in Cardiff and Barry docks discharging cargoes. They were sent to the Rhondda for military training to prepare them for the task awaiting them during the invasion, which was the responsibility of ensuring the safe transportation of equipment and materials from the ships across the beaches and on to dry land. They had already been sent to assault training centres in Devon and near the Mumbles to train in amphibious operations. They were in the Rhondda to increase their fitness and to practise with their weapons at the firing range at Treforest.

The mountains above the valleys were already being used as training grounds for infantry divisions. A permanent tented camp was set up in the basin of Craig-y-Llyn, north of Treherbert, the last major conurbation in the Rhondda Fawr. The lake is backed by precipitous cliffs which were probably used for scaling as a training exercise. During this time the whole area was an exclusion zone with road blocks manned by armed guards.

The Americans worked hard on their allotted tasks and in training. As the build up to D-Day began they found themselves undertaking twelve-hour shifts. The work side of their time in Britain is often forgotten. They also played hard, and had a major impact on the social scene. The popularity of dance halls increased and they brought with them the swing music of Glen Miller and the big band sound of Tommy Dorsey. Accompanying the music were exciting new dances such as the jitterbug and the jive. The majority of the Americans were in their late teens or early twenties. The local girls found them attractive and vice versa. Whirlwind romances took place, many of which led to marriages. In Dennis Sellwood's book on Caerphilly there are several sources citing marriages of over fifty years standing. Some liaisons were short, but with long-lasting consequences in terms of the birth of a child and many marriages did not work out, especially when the glamour of the individual was not always reflected in their home town or family. After the war there was an exodus of GI brides to the US. Of the 40,000 women who made this journey it is estimated that about 2,000 were from Wales.

The young children in the communities where the Americans were based found their presence exciting. They brought with them sweets, bubble gum and comics, of which the young soldiers gave generously. The inquisitiveness of some children, however, led to tragedy in Treforest. Three boys investigating the firing range there came across an unexploded grenade. In the ensuing accident one was killed and the others were badly injured.

The young men in the communities were not as enamoured as the women with the presence of the young Americans. Many were miners who had had no choice but to work in that industry which was a reserved occupation by this time. They did not have the wealth that the young Americans were able to flaunt. There were several instances of fights breaking out in Pontypridd. There were also cases of groups of Americans fighting each other. When this happened they were dealt with by their military policemen who used a degree of violence that British policemen were unaccustomed to.

There was one aspect of the American influx that was found concerning and unwelcome. Many of the American soldiers were black. Perhaps for the first time people in Wales witnessed segregation and racism. The black soldiers were in separate units from the white men and lived in separate quarters. Dennis Morgan's account of Cardiff during the war refers to some events in the city. He cites an example of black GIs drinking coffee in a cafe being ordered out when a white officer came in. The cafe manager, to his credit, told the officer that the policy of the cafe was to treat all customers alike. In another incident a black soldier was shot dead in Bute Street, attempting to flee from two military policemen. He had disobeyed orders not to go into Butetown.

Butetown was one of the few areas in the whole of Britain where there was a semblance of a multi-racial society. At the start of the war there were probably only about 8,000 members of the black community in Britain.

Butetown was one of its centres. Many black Americans forged close ties with people in the community and some, stationed in other parts of the country, spent their leave there to avoid any hostility from their fellow GIs.

The departure of the Americans was sudden. During May 1944 soldiers, sailors, ships and equipment began to descend into the ports along the south coast of England and along the Bristol Channel. On the evening of 30 May news was received in the Rhondda that the troops were to be leaving the next day. The scenes in the Empire Cinema, Tonypandy were quite dramatic. Mrs Verdun Lucas is quoted in Bryan Morse's book.

> The film suddenly stopped and a message was flashed on screen that all American personnel were to report to their depots immediately. The hall lights went on and there were many American soldiers in the audience. They started to rush to the exits urged on by the military police standing in the doorways; there was a general air of disquiet if not panic. Many of the girlfriends of the soldiers became very distressed and some hysterical.
>
> Stationary among the crowd milling about were large Army trucks with their engines running ... some of the girlfriends were still creating a scene and clinging to the soldiers. I heard the military police shout, 'Enough of that' and ordered the men into the trucks. Then, crowded with soldiers they moved slowly until they were clear of the throng , then picked up speed and were gone.

Many were taken to the south coast ports of England in readiness for the crossing to Omaha beach in Normandy. Others were taken to the South Wales Bristol Channel ports. These ports were used in the follow up phase to the initial invasion on 6 June. In the early days of June they were packed with ships and played a critical role in the months that followed in the supply of equipment to the invasion forces.

No sooner had some soldiers left South Wales than they returned as casualties of war. Many had horrific injuries and were taken to the US military hospital at Rhydlafar on the outskirts of Cardiff.

## Refugees, Internees and Prisoners of War

During 1938 and the early months of 1939 school log books for some Cardiff schools recorded the admittance of a small number of refugee children from Austria and Czechoslovakia. These young people, mainly Jewish, were a sign of the war to come. They followed the Basque children from northern Spain, who had fled from the victorious fascist forces of General Franco in 1938 and were accommodated in Caerleon, Swansea, Brechfa and Old Colwyn. Victims of the bombing of civilian targets in Spain, their experiences were soon to be replicated along the South Wales coast.

There was already a tradition of Wales being a haven for refugees dating back to the First World War, when a group of Belgians had settled in Cardiff. The Second World War saw another generation arriving in 1940. As Hitler swept through the Low Countries during May of that year numbers of Dutch and Belgian refugees escaped in fishing boats from the ports and eventually found their way to Cardiff, where a community of approximately 500 were to stay until 1945. Belgian troops who were evacuated from Dunkirk were directed to regroup along with other Belgians who were already in the country and were assigned to Tenby. They were designated as the Belgian Combat Unit. They later moved to Carmarthen and eventually became known as the Belgian Liberation Brigade. They fought their way home via the Normandy Landings of 1944.

As Hitler's troops advanced into France from Belgium, Mussolini, who had kept Italy neutral since the beginning of the war, chose to commit his forces in support of Hitler. On 10 June he declared war on Britain and France and sent his troops into the south eastern corner of France. This had significant consequences for the Italian community that had been established in Wales since the early part of the twentieth century. Mussolini's invasion was met with a spontaneous reaction in parts of South Wales. Angry crowds gathered outside Italian-owned cafes in Swansea and Cardiff, and at one demonstration outside a cafe in Grangetown, Cardiff, the police had to be called to disperse the protesters. In some towns such as Neath, the authorities closed down the cafes and a round up of Italians of military age began. The story of the Italian community in South Wales has been told by Colin Hughes in his book *Lime, Lemon and Sarsparilla*.

The majority of Italians in South Wales originated from the town of Bardi and the surrounding area, the Ceno Valley, in north-east Italy. They had settled in the Welsh towns and villages, and their cafes were common meeting places. Overnight, however, they became 'enemy aliens'. The government had plans to divide the 'aliens' into three categories – those posing a high security risk, doubtful cases and those deemed to pose no risk at all. These categories would be assessed at tribunals. June 1940, however, was an unusual time, with the fear of imminent invasion a very real threat. Orders from Churchill came to 'collar the lot'. By the middle of June all men of Italian nationality aged between sixteen and seventy were interned. Across South Wales several hundred homes received a knock on the door that was to lead to the breaking up of families and in some cases tragedy. The arrests were largely done in a sympathetic manner with both the police and the Italians equally bemused.

Once arrested the Italians were placed in temporary detention centres such as Maindy barracks in Cardiff. They were then moved to camps in Lancashire where conditions were cramped and unhygienic. A decision was then taken to send some of the internees to Canada, others to Australia and the rest to the Isle of Man.

On 1 July 1940 the *Arandora Star*, a cruise liner, left Liverpool for Canada with over 1,500 German and Italian internees. At 7am on 2 July, whilst sailing 125 miles north-west of Ireland, it was hit by a torpedo from a German U-boat; 486 Italians and 175 Germans lost their lives. Amongst the Italians there were over forty from South Wales. Today forty-nine men, who came from the Ceno Valley, are remembered on a plaque in a small chapel in the cemetery at Bardi. Of these at least thirty-nine were arrested in South Wales. Two other Welsh-based Italians are also remembered on a separate plaque in Bardi.

How particular individuals came to be on the *Arandora Star* is an unresolved mystery. The intention was that they should be those who were active supporters of the views of Mussolini, but it appears that very few were fascists and that the main factor that linked them was that they had not become British citizens. The list of Italians whose removal from Britain was considered to be desirable came from MI5. Colin Hughes quotes the evidence of Sir Percy Loraine, who was head of a Home Office Advisory Committee set up after the sinking of the *Arandora Star* to consider the release of Italian internees on the Isle of Man, to explain how individuals may have found themselves on the MI5 list and how unrealistic it was. In an early briefing from the Foreign Office Loraine was told that MI5 were of the view that there was an Italian fascist secret society in existence in which every member was actively engaged in sabotage and fifth column activities. Under cross-examination MI5 had admitted that they were largely influenced in their attitude by the fear of invasion and that they had no evidence of subversive activities beyond membership of the *Fascio*. Following interviews with internees, Loraine discovered the true meaning, for many, of membership of the *Fascio*.

> A man who belonged in the pre-Fascist era to an Italian benevolent, social or sporting club, of which the Fascist authority ultimately gained control, is only technically, indeed barely technically, a member of the Fascio.

Colin Hughes concludes, therefore, that some Italians in Wales were members of the Fascist Party by default. Many cafe owners were members of trade organisations which were taken over by the *Fascio* and others, veterans of the First World War, were members of the Italian Legion which was also taken over.

On 24 August 1940 Regional Civil Defence commissioners were instructed to prepare a 'suspect list' of potential traitors and collaborators in the event of enemy invasion. These lists were not revealed until the end of 2004. On the Welsh list there were a number of Italians who were identified as being active members of the Italian Fascist Party; one had trained with the Italian Army, others were accused of intimidating naturalised British subjects of Italian origin and others of communicating with foreign seamen. Undoubtedly, therefore, there were members of the Italian community who were inclined towards fascism. On the other hand the majority of those who died on the *Arandora Star* or found themselves deported to internment camps in Canada and Australia or spent most of the war years on the Isle of Man, were innocent individuals in the wrong place at the wrong time, victims of paranoia created by war.

Mussolini's decision to join with Hitler brought his troops into conflict with British troops in North Africa. In December 1940 the British attacked and defeated the Italians at Sidi Barrani on the Libyan/Egyptian border. Over 40,000 prisoners of war were taken. By February 1941, there were over 133,000 Italian prisoners of war following further British victories at Bardia and Tobruk. Success on this scale, whilst Britons at home were suffering the horrors of the Blitz, was a boost to morale. It also brought some problems. Up to this point the number of prisoners of war in Britain had been limited to Luftwaffe pilots and crew who had crashed or been shot down and naval personnel from ships that had been sunk. A handful of prisoner of war camps had opened, mainly in Scotland and northern England. Wales was an obvious location as the demand for more camps increased.

Italian PoWs began to arrive in Britain at the end of 1941. The majority were housed in Nissan hut camps and put to work. This was mainly on farms but the prisoners were also used in timber production, limestone quarrying, repairing roads and clearing bombsites. From a camp in Cefn Mably, east of Cardiff, Italian PoWs worked on farms in the surrounding area. Land Girls working at the Tair Onen Forestry Commission near St Fagans found themselves working alongside them.

The Geneva Convention of 1929 stated that private soldiers could be put to work, provided that it was not of military importance. There was a broad interpretation of this regulation but the Italians were cooperative and relaxed about the arrangements. At the end of the war, of 75,000 Italian PoWs in Britain, a third chose to stay rather than be repatriated. A permanent reminder of their presence exists at Henllan Bridge near Carmarthen, where the prisoners built a chapel and created a fresco of the Last Supper.

The majority of PoWs in Wales and Britain before 1944 were Italian. In June 1944 there were 7,900 Germans in Britain. The number of German PoWs was to increase significantly following the Normandy landings and, as a result, the number of PoW camps. Historical research on prisoner of war camps has been relatively recent. A report for English Heritage by Dr Anthony Hellen has identified twenty-three in Wales; some were hostels from which the prisoners went out to work on farms, some were work camps and others were medical centres:

Island Farm, Bridgend
Claremont, Abergavenny
Anglesey
Greenfield Farm, Presteign
Henllan Bridge Camp, Llandyssul
Glandulas Camp, Newtown
Llandarrog Camp, Carmarthenshire
Maerdy Camp, Abergavenny
Pabo Hall Camp, Llandudno Junction
Llanmartin Camp, Magor

The Mount, Chepstow
Ystrad Camp, Carmarthen
Haverfordwest
Llanover Park, Abergavenny
Talgarth Hospital
Abergwili Hospital, Carmarthen
Abbey Road, Neath
Swanbridge, Sully
Penclawdd, Swansea
Pendre Camp, Builth Wells
New Inn Camp, Pontypool
Royal Artillery Practice Camp, Sennybridge
Ordnance Storage Depot, Queensferry

Little is known about the majority of the camps and Dr Hellen has identified some broad areas for future research, including how, where and when prisoners were held, the billeting of prisoners on farms, the importance of PoW labour to food production and the role played by the camps in the reconciliation process.

There is one exception to this gap in knowledge – Island Farm, Bridgend – due to the momentous event that occurred on the night of 10/11 of March 1945 when sixty-seven German prisoners tunnelled their way to freedom. The full story has been told in the work by Herbert Williams, *Come Out, Wherever You Are*, first published in 1976 and republished in 2004; and by Peter Phillips, who has told the story in the wider context of the events of the war in his book *The Great German Escape*.

The capture of German prisoners created new issues for the British authorities. They included different types of prisoners. Many were officers and many were hard line Nazis. New PoW camps had to be built, some with high security.

The German prisoners were graded at three levels. The 'White' grade indicated that they were anti-Nazi and could possibly be persuaded to work with the Allies, the 'Grey' grade were those who were loyal to Germany, but did not have an unfailing allegiance to Hitler and the 'Black' grade were those who were diehard supporters of Hitler, many of whom were in the SS. By and large there was a separation of officers from other ranks, although some members of the lower ranks served officers and some officers were put in charge of their subordinates.

The first inmates that came to Island Farm were mainly a mixture of low-ranking Italian and German prisoners. One of their main tasks was to erect a perimeter fence for greater security. They were replaced in November 1944 by a group of 1,600 Germans, mainly officers, including a significant number of SS men. The attitude of many members of this group was very different from that of previous inmates. According to Herbert Williams the younger ones were particularly bellicose and set out to taunt and intimidate their guards, a group of soldiers medically downgraded due to illness or injury.

The attitude of the Germans was demonstrated on their arrival at Bridgend railway station. Herbert Williams wrote that 'they came, in fact, not like defeated men, but like conquerors'. They lined up on the station platform and sang their national anthem *'Deutschland Uber Alles'*. They then proceeded to march through the town to the prison camp singing songs such as 'We Will Fight and Die for the Führer'. Amongst their number were officers from Operation Todt, the civil engineering organisation responsible for reconstruction projects in Nazi-controlled countries. Their presence was of great significance as they had the skills and knowledge to support the tunnel building operation that led to the escape of the prisoners on 10/11 March 1945.

The tunnel was planned with precision. Sixty feet long, it emerged ten feet on the outside of the perimeter fence. The technical know-how of some of the inmates meant it had a lighting system and a system for providing the tunnelers with air.

Over approximately a five-hour period sixty-seven of the inmates escaped. The last one to emerge, however, was seen racing from the escape hatch to some trees and was shot in the shoulder. As guards arrived at the scene a further ten were discovered in the surrounding area and gave themselves up. This left fifty-six at large. There began a major manhunt which involved hundreds of local volunteers, the police, soldiers and airmen from the RAF base at St Athan.

On the Monday evening the police inspector leading the operation to track down the escapees received a telephone call informing him that a woman had been shot at nearby Porthcawl. It was believed that the culprit was one of the Germans on the run. The shooting was to turn into a murder enquiry which had to be addressed at the same time as the man hunt. This added to the challenge of trying to calm the locals, which was not helped by newspaper headlines such as

'SS Men in Mass Tunnel Getaway' and ' Escaped Nazis Plan Sabotage'. The murderer turned out to be a Canadian Army deserter who had killed his lover and initially used the breakout as the explanation when reporting the shooting.

As the week went on, not only did the murder mystery unravel but many of the prisoners were caught. The vast majority were found within the county of Glamorgan, including thirty within seven miles of the camp. Four made it to within a mile of Birmingham airport having travelled 130 miles. Another two reached Eastleigh, near Southampton, 150 miles away, having journeyed mostly on a train carrying ammunition. Two more were caught close to the Severn Tunnel in Monmouthshire. The final three were arrested on the Saturday following the breakout, having tasted freedom for nearly a week.

At the end of March all 1,600 prisoners at Island Farm were dispersed to other prison camps across Britain. It was not the end of the story for Island Farm as a prison camp. In January 1946 it reopened to receive the elite of the German Army including field marshals, generals and admirals. Amongst these was Field Marshal von Runstedt, commander of the German forces on the western front until his replacement two months before the end of the war. Also at Island Farm was Walter Dornberger, a scientist who had helped Werner von Braun on the development of the V1 and V2 rockets that had caused such devastation over southeast England in the last phase of the war. He was headhunted by the Americans and worked with von Braun on their space programme.

During the week of the Island Farm escape many newspaper articles critical of the authorities were written. One view to emerge was that the prisoners had been treated too well, as some had been caught with a reasonable stock of food. It was a theme that political cartoonists linked to the incarceration of the most prominent Nazi to be detained in Wales, Rudolf Hess, Hitler's former deputy. It was believed that Hess was being held in luxurious circumstances. A *News of the World* cartoon shows Hess reading a newspaper at a table which has a bowl of fruit, a bottle of wine and a menu on it. Emerging from the floor are four characters with pickaxes and shovels. The caption reads, 'Pst, Rudolf, we've tunnelled our way over – what's for lunch?'

Hess was in South Wales from 26 June 1942 until 8 October 1945. For most of this time he was at the PoW reception station at Maindiff Court near Abergavenny. It also appears that he spent some time at Cefn

Mably which was an interrogation centre, and at Porth Mawr Mansion, Crickhowell. Maindiff Court was formerly the home of the Ironmaster, Crawshay Bailey which probably explains why it was thought that he was being held in the lap of luxury. Whilst at Maindiff Court it appears that Hess had a degree of freedom. He was not confined entirely to the house. It is said that he walked the surrounding hills, including the Sugar Loaf, accompanied by armed guards, and a favourite activity of his was to feed swans in the moat at White Castle.

The full story of Rudolf Hess will not be known until 2017 at least, when the British records about him are due to be released. He claimed that he flew to Scotland in 1941 on a peace mission. After a period of detention in Scotland he was eventually moved to the Tower of London and then to a barracks in Aldershot. Whilst there a Polish soldier broke into the building and attempted to assassinate him. Following this attack he was moved to South Wales.

Once the war was over many prisoners of war chose to remain in Wales and they were joined by soldiers and refugees from countries that had been conquered by Hitler during the war, such as Poland and Czechoslovakia. Their countries had been taken over by Communist regimes allied to the Soviet Union. These people had little desire to return home, especially as their flight from their homeland may have been interpreted as an act of desertion which the new governments would seek to punish.

## Chapter Seven

# June 1944 – July 1945:
# Victory over Germany, Labour
# Victory at Home

From the last months of 1942 the nature of the military presence in Wales changed. Until then the RAF and the Royal Navy had had a predominantly defensive role, protecting coastal waters, the naval convoys with their essential supplies and vulnerable military targets on land such as airfields and munitions factories. The air force did take part in occasional sorties against enemy airfields and ports in France and soldiers trained in Wales did move on to the arenas of war, but primarily the military presence was defensive.

Preparations geared towards a military offensive against Germany took significant steps forward during 1942. The plan was for a British, Canadian and American force to invade occupied France across the English Channel. Wales played an important role in the planning and preparations in several respects. Factories and specialist production sites made equipment and armaments for the invading forces, the ports along the Bristol Channel became massive storage areas for the equipment and supplies needed for the invasion and tracts of rough and mountainous terrain became the training ground for troops preparing for the assault on the enemy.

One particular area of Wales made a unique contribution to the plans for the Normandy landings. Allied commanders realised that an invasion force would need constant backup once the initial landings of troops had taken place. Further landings of troops would be needed and a constant flow of supplies including more military equipment, technical support and food. As the capture of a port was not guaranteed in the early days of an assault it was decided to construct a prefabricated harbour off the Normandy coast. Within the harbour, pierheads, floating quays, were built to provide stable platforms onto which the ships could unload their cargos. From the pierheads, floating roadways extended to the coast to enable convoys of lorries to take the supplies to land. On the day after D-Day the sections of the artificial harbours were towed out across the English Channel and then constructed off the Normandy coast. It was an engineering feat of epic proportions.

Early in 1941 a Welsh civil engineer, Iorys Hughes, had sent ideas to the War Office about the construction of artificial harbours. In June 1942, on the instructions of Winston Churchill, he was contacted and requested to produce more detailed proposals. He was then given a contract to build and test his prototype. Iorys Hughes was a native of Bangor. As a young man he had had a great interest in sailing. He knew the North Wales coastline well, including Conway and the Conway Estuary. He thought that a section of land called Morfa would be an ideal building site for his project. The land was owned by Conway Town Council, which was informed that the Prime Minister himself regarded the work to be carried out on the land as being high priority. Work started in November 1942 and many buildings nearby were taken over to provide accommodation for workmen. None of the workmen, including the management, were aware of what they were building.

The prototype was ready by June 1943. The parts were towed to the Solway Firth in Scotland to be tested. Two other prototypes were also tested. Although his exact design was not chosen, many of Iorys Hughes' ideas were adapted to the chosen model and he was kept on as a consultant. Work on building the Mulberry Harbours, as they became known, began in December 1943. Conway was one of sixteen construction sites around the country used to build the components. By the beginning of May 1944, after huge efforts by 900 men, six pierheads had been constructed on the Morfa site and were ready to be transferred to assembly points on the south coast of England. The contribution made by the town of Conway to the winning of the war was not widely known. The story has recently been told by Mark Hughes in his book *Conwy Mulberry Harbour*.

In addition to this specific contribution to the Normandy landings, Wales had other attributes that supported the operation, such as beaches. The coastal town of Tywyn witnessed the arrival of numbers of amphibious landing craft during 1943, as the Tywyn estuary with a range of different types of beach was an ideal practice ground for the landings. Further south around Carmarthen Bay, a full-scale exercise known as Operation Jantzen took place in July 1943 as part of the preparations for the invasion of Europe.

An account of Operation Jantzen appears in a short booklet called *Tenby during World War Two* by John Tipton. He describes how for a brief period the town took on some of the characteristics of an occupied territory. Restrictions were imposed along the coast from Tenby to Laugharne and inland to a depth of six miles. Entry into the regulated area was denied to all non-residents. Tenby was placed under curfew from dusk until dawn, civilians were not allowed to carry cameras, telescopes or binoculars and had to have their identity cards with them at all times. Civilian mail, telegraph and telephones were subjected to censorship. Control points were set up on all roads and railway stations leading into the area. The press was successfully censored, although this did not stop speculation that the invasion of Europe was about to take place.

The aim of the exercise was to practice beach maintenance for the landing of an armed force and their supply over a period of fourteen days. Port Talbot, Swansea and Tenby were designated 'friendly' territory from which the 'invasion' was launched. The 'enemy' beaches were between Pendine and Saundersfoot. The logistics of loading and unloading supply ships from different types of vessels under different conditions were all noted in preparation for Operation Overlord, the invasion of Normandy. There are unconfirmed reports that both Winston Churchill and General Eisenhower – Commander-in-Chief of the Allied Forces – came to the area to observe the operation. Churchill is reputed to have visited the Inn at Wiseman's Bridge.

In the immediate months prior to the D-Day landings there was an enormous amount of activity building up to the invasion. Dennis Morgan describes how the open space to the east of the Queen Alexandra Dock in Cardiff became known as the 'Prairie' as it filled up with American vessels, guns, tanks, vehicles, bombs and shells.

An account of the planning for D Day was released to the public in March 1945. The operation was described as 'probably the first overseas military expedition to sail from South Wales'. The Germans expected a full-scale invasion from the south coast of England, the Welsh dimension of the invasion contributed to the element of surprise.

Almost half of the merchant shipping sent to support the Allied landings in France sailed from the Bristol Channel ports. Practically every Welsh-owned coaster was commandeered for the operation. For many months before the invasion all ship repairing and shipbuilding resources in the area were engaged in constructing, fitting out and adapting a considerable number of ships and landing craft. Two divisions of the United States Army, with their vehicles and equipment, sailed from the Bristol Channel ports and arrived in the assault area on 6 and 7 June 1944. The original date for sailing was 5 June, but a heavy gale began to blow in the Bristol Channel and orders were received postponing the operation for twenty-four hours.

One of the most remarkable features of the D Day operation was that it was accomplished with so much secrecy. When part of the convoy was assembling off Barry, Barry Island and its leisure facilities were closed to the public for a week. Although the masters of all merchant vessels taking part were briefed at convoy conferences they did not know their exact destination until they opened a sealed envelope at an appointed place off the south coast of England. The security and secrecy was maintained by thousands of workmen in the ports.

The D-Day landings took place early in the morning of 6 June 1944. As he went to bed on the night before Churchill told his wife: 'by the time you wake up in the morning 20,000 men may have been killed'. Amongst the invading forces on the first day were the 2nd/24th Battalion of the South Wales Borderers who were the only Welsh battalion to land on the Normandy beaches on D-Day itself. Others were soon to follow, and out of the South Wales ports, in particular, came the supplies needed to sustain the invasion.

Amongst the Welshmen who landed on the beaches was the late historian Gwyn Alf Williams. In *Fishers of Men: Stories Towards an Autobiography*, he described his journey from a landing craft into the sea, across a beach and up a hill. At the top of the hill,

I turned back – and was suddenly seized with a terrible exultation … The scene opened up in a breath-taking panorama. The whole sea seemed full of ships; you could have walked back to Newhaven on the decks. Thousands of men were pouring ashore, milling around the beach, tanks leading them off. Over our heads was a continuous roar and the sky was dark with aircraft. The sheer impact of all that mass of men, material, aircraft and ships was overwhelming. I stood there astounded. It was one of my two historic moments.

Back in Swansea there was an equally amazed ten-year-old youngster. Brian Owen recalls a sight that made a lasting impression upon him in *Memories of Mumbles at War*. As he was cycling from Murton to Brynmill in Swansea, 'Swansea Bay came into sight, just before reaching the top of the Mayals, I couldn't believe my eyes. The bay was packed with hundreds of ships.'

The D-Day landings were the beginning of a long drawn out conclusion to the final defeat of Hitler. Much blood was to be shed before VE Day on 8 May 1945.

The Normandy campaign saw the first Welsh soldier receive a Victoria Cross. It went to a remarkable character, described in his later life as 'the greatest living Welshman'. Sir Tasker Watkins died in 2007 aged eighty-eight, having had a distinguished legal career, been President of the Welsh Rugby Union for thirteen years and held a number of important administrative posts. In August 1944 he was a lieutenant in the 1/5th Battalion of the Welsh Regiment. He was an officer in a group leading an assault on a Nazi machine-gun post. Whilst advancing through a booby-trapped cornfield all the other officers were killed. Lieutenant Watkins then led the remaining thirty men in a bayonet charge against fifty enemy infantry, practically wiping them out. He then single-handedly took out the machine-gun post and went on to lead his men back to safety.

Watkins came from the village of Nelson in the Rhymney Valley. Remarkably the only other Welsh soldier to receive the Victoria Cross also came from the valley. This was Corporal Edward Chapman from Pontlottyn. Chapman had taken part in the D-Day landings as a member of the Monmouthshire Regiment. He was wounded in the fighting and spent six weeks in hospital recovering. He then joined the regiment again for the invasion of Germany. In April 1945 they were in an area of northern Germany called Teutoberger Wald which was defended by a battalion of German officer cadets and their instructors who were fanatical Nazis. Corporal Chapman's section was advancing in single file along a narrow path when the enemy opened fire with machine-guns at short range, inflicting heavy casualties. Corporal Chapman ordered his section to take cover, seized a Bren gun and advanced alone firing the gun from his hip, mowing down the enemy at point-blank range. They retired in disorder but then regrouped and made a bayonet charge towards Chapman who 'again rose with his Bren gun to meet the assaults, and again halted their advance'. As his company retreated Chapman carried his injured commander back to safety in the face of 'withering fire'. Unfortunately, the officer died.

In 1988 Edward Chapman was interviewed by schoolteacher Philip Tapper who asked him why he did it:

> Well, you had to do it … the men in my section were youngsters, they were so raw … At that time I was twenty-five years old, but all of the men in my section were eighteen year olds without much training … they would do what any experienced man asked them to do …

Philip Tapper undertook a series of interviews to show the wide range of experiences during the war, which provided the basis of a booklet for school children called *Voices*. One of his themes was that 'war takes men and women from their homes, and puts them into places and situations they would never have dreamt of.' His interviews with a number of other combatants illustrate this. Amongst them was Les Lewis of Pontycymmer, a sailor who joined the Royal Navy in May 1940. Les joined a branch of the navy known as DEMS (Defensibly Equipped Merchant Ships). He was a one of the military personnel who sailed on merchant ships with responsibility for their defence. On his first journey he sailed to West Africa; he then travelled back and forth across the Atlantic with convoys a number of times, went to India from Liverpool on a troopship, transferred to a cargo ship that carried supplies for the Allied invasion of Italy and then served on a tanker taking supplies to British ships in the Pacific, engaged in the war with Japan. His was truly a 'world' war.

Another interviewee was Roy Perry from the Rhondda Valley, a soldier in the Royal Electrical and Mechanical Engineers. He was captured by the Germans on the island of Crete. After a short time in a prison in Greece he was taken to Germany to a prison camp near Berlin. Later he was moved to another camp in Bavaria where he spent three years. In 1945 after the Allies had invaded Germany and the Americans were getting close, the SS arrived and ordered everyone to march away from the camp. They were forced to march for three weeks until one day the German guards disappeared and shortly afterwards American soldiers arrived to release them. During the forced march they

> ... saw a column coming down from the hilltop, very slowly, from a nearby concentration camp ... there must have been about a hundred of them, in a terrible state, they could hardly walk, they were gaunt like you see in the films of concentration camps ... dressed in striped pyjamas. They made gestures for food to us ... we didn't have any to give them ... At the end of this column was this cart, and as they were dropping, falling and dying, they were putting them on this cart.

Roy had witnessed the horror of the victims of the Holocaust. As the Allied troops liberated France, Belgium and Holland and invaded Germany they became aware of the victims of merciless atrocities. On 15 April 1945 troops liberated the notorious Belsen concentration camp. Sister (Lieutenant) Lucy Edwards from Cwmparc was one of eight British nurses attached to a casualty station near the camp. This is what she told the *Rhondda Leader* on her return home:

> The scene in the camp beggared description. There were approximately 50,000 human beings there, of whom nearly 10,000 lay dead. Those who still breathed had had no food or water for about seven days. Typhus and other diseases raged, and filth everywhere poisoned the air.

War exposed people who had led ordinary lives to unimaginable horrors. The impact of their experiences never left them, although they rarely wished to speak of what they had witnessed.

There is a story for every soldier, sailor, airman and nurse who found themselves in parts of the world they had never dreamt of, doing things that they never expected that they would be doing. Not everyone would perform acts of valour on the scale of Tasker Watkins and Edward Chapman, but thousands upon thousands found untapped resources that enabled them to endure the trials and tribulations of war. Sometimes acts of heroism went unacknowledged at the time, but later their stories came to light. In the 1970s Colonel D.G. Davies-Scourneld wrote a newspaper article under the title, 'The Bravest Welshman I have known'. He referred to Frank Goodwin, a Crosville bus conductor from Gwersyllt, near Wrexham. Frank was a lance-sergeant with the 3rd Battalion of the Welsh Guards. In May 1944 they were in Italy advancing towards Rome. His men came under fire from an enemy machine-gun post. He ordered them to take cover and ran across exposed country towards the enemy fire, firing his Bren-gun from the hip. On running out of bullets he threw his weapon to the ground and continued to advance, hurling hand grenades at the enemy position. Eventually the machine-gun fell silent. Goodwin's men broke cover. When they arrived at the enemy position Frank Goodwin lay dead, his body draped over the machine-gun encircled by German casualties. On 2 January 1972, the popular boys comic, *The Victor* told Frank's story in picture form.

When the war with Germany came to a close in May 1945, the war against Japan continued. There were many Welsh troops in the Far East still fighting for the next three months. Battalions from the South Wales Borderers, the Welch Regiment and the Royal Welsh Fusiliers were all in Burma. Those that were to suffer the most harrowing experiences were probably the soldiers that fought in Burma and the men women and children that found themselves in Japanese prisoner of war camps where disease, starvation and humiliation were commonplace.

Amongst those imprisoned by the Japanese were members of the 77th Heavy 'Ack-Ack' Regiment of the Royal Artillery which had been raised and trained in Cardiff and the surrounding area. The battalion was led by Lieutenant-Colonel H.R. Humphries who had been a telephone engineer in Cardiff before the war. He had about 1,000 men under his command. They fought for six weeks against the Japanese in Java, before they were taken prisoner in March 1942. Over 300 of them were to die in captivity. In September 1945 the surviving 200 men and eleven officers were met by a *Western Mail* reporter called Victor Lewis at the notorious Changi Prisoner of War camp, near Singapore, as they waited to return home. He told their story in a series of three dispatches. At first they were detained at the Gladok Prisoner of War camp in filthy conditions with little to eat but rice, served from coal bags. Some died of starvation and more died of diseases such as beri-beri, cholera and malaria. There were no medical supplies. In May 1943 the prisoners were split up and sent to gaols throughout the Far East. Humphries was sent into the Burmese jungle in charge of 3,500 men including 300 from his own regiment to build a railway. He came back with 886, due to further losses through disease and starvation and in some cases death as a result of savage beatings. Throughout this dreadful period and in the face of appalling conditions and ill-treatment they worked hard to keep up their spirits and maintain morale. They also maintained their Welsh identity by holding their own *eisteddfodau*.

Fighting in the Far East was an ordeal in itself. Stan Martins from near Bridgend has entered a detailed account on a BBC website. He describes the seven-day crossing of India from Bombay to Calcutta on a troop train. There was no water and no toilet. Men ate, slept and did their ablutions in their carriage. The toilet was a metre square hole in the middle of the compartment. It was stinking hot and the train was literally lousy; Most were covered bites. At first he was employed in the fortification of an air base 200 miles to the south of Calcutta. The base was in a large clearing surrounded by dense jungle teaming with wildlife, especially 'nasties' such as scorpions, centipedes, snakes and flies 'by the million'. Jackals surrounded the camp, howling through the night. It was nothing to find a snake coiled up in a bed or a scorpion inside boots left on the floor. The legs of beds had to stand in water to prevent white ants from eating them. Temperatures were over 100 degrees and the men were soaked with sweat from morning till night. Occasionally there were thunderstorms which left six inches of water in a short period of time. It would rise up and then subside as quickly as it came.

In April 1944 the Japanese invaded north-east India and were defeated at the Battle of Kohima. By this time Stan had joined the Royal Welch Fusiliers and had undertaken a few weeks of intensive infantry training. After Kohima he joined the forces that chased the Japanese back into Burma. At one stage they covered 110 miles in ten days. In addition to the hazards of heat, shortage of water and the need to carry heavy loads, there was the danger of booby traps left behind by the Japanese, the disruption of felled trees across the roads and the threat of ambush from snipers who had been left behind to delay the advance.

The Royal Welch Fusiliers in the Burma campaign evidently took advantage of the ability of many men to speak Welsh. They arranged that one radio operator in every company should be Welsh speaking, so that orders and information could be sent quickly and safely – the Japanese could only intercept messages in English.

By the end of the war 15,000 Welsh service personnel had died and many suffered injuries or traumas from which they never fully recovered. Whilst VE Day was a day of sad remembrance for many who had lost loved ones, it was also a day of huge rejoicing. Below is an extract from an article in the *Rhondda Leader* that captures the spirit of the time, which was replicated across the country.

> When VE Day was officially announced the inhabitants of the two Rhondda Valleys could hardly realise that it was true ... People were quiet and undemonstrative at first, but when full realisation came there was deep gratitude ... Churches were open throughout the valleys and thanksgiving services held were attended by thousands of people.
>
> Later the population began to make whoopee. Streets from one end of the urban area to the other were gaily festooned with streamers, flags, bunting and fairy lights.
>
> Parties were organised and bonfires glowed from hilltop to hilltop. Community singing by large crowds echoed up and down the valleys, and the grand old Welsh hymns and popular songs were sung with buoyancy and true 'hwyl'.
>
> Effigies of Hitler were suspended from lamp posts, and many of them were hung, drawn and quartered or burned with profound pleasure. Every district had its street teas for the children, who had the time of their lives.

The end of the war signalled the end of the coalition government. On 21 May the Labour Party withdrew from the coalition and Churchill continued in power with a 'caretaker' government. An election was called for 5 July, with the result being delayed until 26 July to ensure that ballot papers from service personnel overseas were collected and added into the vote.

It had been known for some time that there would be an election at the end of the war. Churchill had announced the fact in October 1944. From this time on, despite the continuance of the military campaign in Western Europe, partisan speech making began to be a more common feature on the domestic political scene. It was something that Aneurin Bevan had being doing throughout the war. In 1944, under the pseudonym of Celticus, he wrote a book entitled *Why Not Trust the Tories*, in which he demanded alternative domestic policies based on socialist principles and public ownership of industry. The book sold over 80,000 copies. It recounted the post-war story following the First World War and drew the lessons to be learned following the end of the Second.

These lessons were provided by others too. An equally as significant figure amongst Welsh Labour Party MPs was James Griffiths, the representative for Llanelli. It was his amendment that had led to the revolt of Labour MPs against the decision of the coalition government to delay implementation of the Beveridge Report until after the end of the war. He was also an important member of the Welsh Advisory Panel of the Ministry of Reconstruction that published a report in 1944 that called for Wales to become recognised as a separate planning unit after the war and for there to be a huge investment into the economy in order to ensure that the social and economic stagnation of the inter-war years should not be repeated.

Since the latter days of 1942 there had been signs that radical change was desired once the war was over. In January 1943 a by-election in the small constituency of the University of Wales had brought the Welsh Nationalist Party back into the limelight of Welsh politics. Saunders-Lewis stood as a candidate and polled 22 per cent of the votes. Much of the debate was concerned with how best the Welsh language and culture should be defended. Since the war had begun issues such as the arrival of evacuees from England; the billeting of English-speaking troops in rural areas; the takeover of Mynydd Epynt and other tracts of land by the War Office; the reduction of radio services in Welsh; and the growing influence of the English medium for entertainment in films and music all threatened the future of the language and culture.

A committee for the defence of the culture of Wales, *Undeb Cymru Fydd*, had been formed early in the war. Whilst it had failed to make an impact in relation to the takeover of Mynydd Epynt, its messages began to be heard. In 1942 the Welsh Courts Act gave legal validity to the use of Welsh in court proceedings, a belated acknowledgement of the argument of Saunders-Lewis, Valentine Williams and D.J. Williams to be tried in their own language in the Penyberth arson case. It was, however, regarded as a meagre step forward by nationalists. Saunders-Lewis's chief opponent in the by-election was Professor W.J. Gruffydd, well-respected poet and champion of Welsh literature. He sought to promote Welsh culture through the universities and established political systems. The defeat of Saunders-Lewis was a defeat for political nationalism, but the campaign raised the profile of his party once more and of issues related to Welsh culture.

A more remarkable feat for the Welsh Nationalist Party, in many ways, was the achievement of Wynne Samuel in the Neath by-election of May

1945. Just over a week after VE Day, he gained 16 per cent of the vote. This was below the percentage achieved by Saunders-Lewis in the University by-election, but this was a predominantly industrial and working class constituency. It was a breakthrough for the WNP which had its main support in north-west Wales and amongst the intelligentsia.

In Neath the coalition candidate was a Labour Party stalwart and gained over 30,000 votes; further east, however, there was a more significant result in terms of the future general election. Bob Edwards, the chairman of the ILP gained 45.5 per cent of the vote in the Newport by-election against a Conservative coalition candidate, 2,702 votes short of victory.

The general election campaign was comparatively quiet at local level, although the speeches of politicians at national level raised the temperature of debate. The result, deemed a surprise, was an overwhelming victory for the Labour Party. Churchill, the war leader, rapturously received by the people as he toured the country following VE Day, was not considered to be the right man to take forward a post-war programme of national reconstruction. Labour received 48.8 per cent of the vote and gained a parliamentary majority of 148. This was somewhat of a miss-match reflecting the vagaries of the British parliamentary system.

In Wales, however, there was no surprise and there was no miss-match. The Labour Party took 58.5 per cent of the vote in Wales, 10 per cent more than that for the United Kingdom. Twenty-five out of thirty-six seats were won, including seven gains. This restored the situation that had pertained in the 1929 General Election. Then, however, Labour had only 43.9 per cent of the vote. In twenty-one of the seats won, Labour had an overall majority. In seven seats the party won over eighty per cent of the vote. In Llanelli, James Griffiths had a majority of 34,000, the largest of any in the country. The main opposition to Labour in Wales came from the Liberal Party who won seven seats, 7/12th of their overall number. The Conservatives won 25 per cent of the vote in Wales. They won seats in anglicised border areas such as Monmouth and Flintshire and areas which had seen an influx of English civil servants such as Caernarfon Boroughs and Denbigh. However, along with east London, Wales was the most anti-Tory part of Britain.

The Labour Party hegemony in the coalfield was maintained, and in one seat, Rhondda West, the MP, Will John was elected unopposed. It made gains in Cardiff, Newport, Barry and Caernarfonshire and only failed to take Anglesey, Merioneth and Pembrokeshire by very small margins. There was a defeat in Carmarthenshire and a near defeat in Rhondda East. Here, however, the challenge came from the left, the Communist Party. The popular Harry Pollitt lost by only 972 votes. This was very much a local circumstance, as the Communist Party had a very strong local organisation and a tradition of challenging the seat.

The massive vote in favour of a Labour government in coalfield areas was no surprise, but Labour's strength extended throughout Wales. However, what was of even greater significance was that the result across Britain which was beyond the party's wildest dreams. It meant that the votes for Labour, which had been for a rump party in 1929 which had no power, were now a part of a much wider phenomenon that could ensure that expectations might be realised. As an act of faith with Wales, an area that had maintained its support for Labour during the bleakest years, responsibility for the two major reforming ministries in the new government, Social Insurance and Health, was given to two South Wales mining MPs, James Griffiths and Aneurin Bevan.

In recent years historians have debated the reasons for the Labour Party's overwhelming victory. Discussion revolves around the extent to which the vote indicated a move towards left wing ideas amongst the electorate or a desire to ensure that the Conservatives were not re-elected. The answer probably lies in there being a mixture of the two. Going back to the parliamentary debate about the Beveridge Report in early 1943 when Labour backbenchers threatened to leave the coalition on a large scale, the Labour Party established itself as the political party most likely to introduce post-war reforms. On the other hand the election campaign provided the opportunity to attack the record of the Conservatives in the 1930s and associate them with the unemployment of that decade. Professor Kenneth Morgan states that the campaign was charged with folk memories and communal bitterness, he concludes that 'the General Election provided a suitable final comment on the ordeal of Wales during the 1920s and 1930s'.

# List of Illustrations

1. Newspaper vendor, the day after war was declared. (*Western Mail*, 4 September 1939/by permission of Media Wales Ltd)

2. Royal Welsh Fusiliers leave Newtown for army camps near the coast just after the declaration of war in September 1939. (By permission of Llyfrgell Genedlaethol Cymru/The National Library of Wales)

3. Young evacuees from Birkenhead arrive at Newtown Station, September 1939. (By permission of Llyfrgell Genedlaethol Cymru/The National Library of Wales)

4. Evacuees at Usk. (*Western Mail*, 2 September 1939/by permission of Media Wales Ltd)

5. Front page of memorial programme to commemorate the deaths of those who died in the bombing of Cwmparc in the Rhondda Valley. Three evacuee children and their mother were killed in the attack. (Courtesy of David Maddox)

6. Children in Montgomeryshire practising putting on their gasmasks in September 1939. In the early part of the war gas masks had to be carried at all times by everyone. (By permission of Llyfrgell Genedlaethol Cymru/The National Library of Wales)

*On 7 September 1940 the German Junker Ju88 was on a reconnaissance mission to the north-west of England. It was spotted and a Spitfire based at Hawarden attacked the plane and took out one of the engines. The Junkers Ju88, now with only one engine, was chased towards mid-Wales and the Spitfire attacked again. The German plane plunged to the ground on a mountainside near Mallwyd. All four airmen on board were badly injured and were taken to Machynlleth Hospital. They survived and were taken to a prisoner of war camp in Canada.*

(From *No Landing Place* by Edward Doylerush)

14. Land reclamation between Machynlleth and Newtown in June 1941. In rural and mountainous areas reclamation was undertaken to increase the amount of land that could be used to grow crops and therefore reduce food shortages. (By permission of Llyfrgell Genedlaethol Cymru/The National Library of Wales)

15. Helping to win the war on the Kitchen Front. The Ministry of Food organised cookery classes and food demonstrations to show people how to improvise and use home-grown produce. This was a class in Newtown in October 1940. (By permission of Llyfrgell Genedlaethol Cymru/The National Library of Wales)

16. A member of the Women's Land Army being given a tractor maintenance test in October 1943. Members had to pass practical and oral tests in a range of subjects, including dairying and dairy work, general farm work, hen breeding, tractor driving, horticulture, fruit production and pest control. (By permission of Llyfrgell Genedlaethol Cymru/The National Library of Wales)

17. David Lloyd George's last public appearance at Caernarvon in April 1940. (By permission of Llyfrgell Genedlaethol Cymru/The National Library of Wales)

David Lloyd George had led the coalition government in the last years of the First World War. In May 1940 he made his last speech in the House of Commons supporting the call for Neville Chamberlain to resign and for a coalition government. In December 1942 he cast his last vote, supporting Labour Party rebels who wanted a commitment that the Beveridge Report recommendations would be introduced before the end of hostilities.

18. Aneurin Bevan's statue in Cardiff. (Courtesy of David Maddox) Bevan is primarily remembered as the founder of the National Health Service. His role as constant critic of the government during the Second World War is little known.

19. J.C. Walker Cartoon, *Western Mail*, 1 September 1943. (By permission of Media Wales Ltd)

Created at the time of the Penrikyber Colliery dispute in September 1943, the cartoon presents an argument against the strikers.

20. The entrance to the cavern in Wales that stored precious art works throughout the war. The *Western Mail* story indicates that this information did not become public knowledge until the end of the war. (*Western Mail*, 5 May 1945/by permission of Media Wales Ltd)

21. Celebrating the end of the war; a street party in Pembroke Dock. (Courtesy of Mrs Joan Watts)

# Bibliography

Beddoe, Deidre, *Out of the Shadows: A History of Women in Twentieth Century Wales* (University of Wales Press, 2000)

Berry, David, *Wales and Cinema* (University of Wales Press, 1984)

Besley, Edward, *For Those in Peril* (National Museum and Galleries, Wales, 2004)

Bowler, Sally, *Swansea at War* (Sutton Publishing, 2006)

Broomfield, Stuart, *Wales between the Wars* (Welsh History Resources Unit, 1986)

Brunning, David, 'Reminiscences of Llantwit Major during World War Two' from *Llantwit Major, Aspects of its History*, Volume 5 (2005)

Calder, Angus, *The Peoples War* (Johnathan Cape, 1969)

Calder, Angus, *Disasters and Heroes* (University of Wales Press, 2004)

Carradice, Philip and Breverton, Terry, *Welsh Sailors of the Second World War* (Glyndwr Publishing, 2007)

Carradice, Philip, *Wales at War* (Gomer Press, 2003)

Carradice, Philip, *Coming Home, Wales after the War* (Gomer Press, 2005)

Coombes, B.L., *Those Clouded Hills* (Cobbett Publishing Co. 1944)

Coombes, B.L., *Miners Day* (Penguin, 1945)

Davies, Hywel D., *The Welsh Nationalist Party, 1925–1945* (Cardiff, 1983)

Davies, John, *A History of Wales* (Allen Lane, The Penguin Press, 1993)

Doylerush, Edward, *Fallen Eagles* (Midlands Counties Publications, 1990)

Doylerush, Edward, *No Landing Place*, Vol. 2 (Midland Publishing, 1999)

Elliot, Kate, Powell, Carol and Powell, John (Eds.), *Memories of Mumbles at War, 1939–1945* (Mumbles Development Trust and Oystermouth Historical Association, 2005)

Foot, Michael, *Aneurin Bevan*, Vol. 1 (MacGibbon and Kee Ltd., 1962)

Gardiner, Juliet, *Wartime Britain, 1939–1945* (Headline Book Publishing, 2004)

HMSO, *When Peace Broke Out – Britain 1945* (HMSO, 1994)

Hughes, Colin, *Lime, Lemon and Sarsparilla* (Seren, 1991)

Hughes, Mark, *Conwy Mulberry Harbour* (Gwaesg Carreg Gwalch, 2001)

Jenkins, Geraint H., *A Concise History of Wales* (Cambridge University Press, 2007)

Jenkins, Philip, *A History of Modern Wales* (Longman, 1992)

Jones, Bill and Williams, Chris (Eds.), *With Dust Still in his Throat: A B.L. Coombes Anthology* (University of Wales Press, 1999)

Jones, Glyndwr G., 'Wartime Caerphilly, Recollections of the years 1939–1945' (*Cronicl Caerfilli* No. 2, 1975)

Jones, Graham J., 'Wales since 1900' from *The Tempus History of Wales, 25,000 BC – AD 2000* (Tempus Publishing, 2001)

Jones, Ivor Wynne, *Hitler's Celtic Echo* (Ivor Wynne Jones, 2006)

Laybourne, Keith, 'England Arise! The General Election of 1945' from *The Historian*, Summer 2005

Lewis Girls Comprehensive School, *Penallta – A Brief History of the Last Working Colliery in the Rhymney Valley* (1994)

Longmate, Norman, *How We Lived Then* (Hutchinson and Co., 1971)

McCamley, N.J., *Saving Britain's Art Treasures* (Lee Cooper, 2003)

McCririck, Mary, *Wales in the Twentieth Century* (Gwasg Gee, 1974)

Morgan, Dennis, *Cardiff: A City at War* (Dennis Morgan, 1998)

Morgan, Kenneth O., *Rebirth of a Nation, Wales 1880–1980* (Oxford University Press, 1981)

Morse, Bryan, *A Moment in Time* (Prospero Books, 2001)

Moseley, Pat, *Ruperra Castle, War and Flames, 1939–1946* (Pat Moseley, 2001)

O'Sullivan, John, *When Wales Went to War* (Sutton Publishing, 2004)

O'Sullivan, John and Bryn Jones, *Cardiff: A Centenary Celebration 1905–2005* (Sutton Publishing, 2005)

Owen, Trefor M., 'Reminiscences of my experiences as a Bevin Boy' from *Llafur* Vol. 9 Number 3, 2003

Pelling, Henry, *Britain and the Second World War* (Fontana, 1970)

Pill, Malcolm, *A Cardiff Family in the Forties* (Morton Priory Press, 1999)

Phillips, Peter, *The German Great Escape* (Seren, 2005)

Powell, Don, *Pontypridd at War 1939–1945* (Morton Priory Press, 1999)

Pritchard, Sydney, *Life in the Welsh Guards, 1939–1946* (Y Lolfa, 2007)

Rhondda Borough Council, *Rhondda Remembers, 1939–1945* (1989)

Roberts, Brian, 'A Mining Town in Wartime: Fears for the Future' from *Llafur* Vol. 6 Number 1, 1992

Sellwood, Dennis G., *The Friendly Invasion* (Caerphilly Local History Society, 2002)

Sloan, Roy, *Anglesey Air Accidents During the Twentieth Century* (Gwasg Carreg Gwalch, 2001)

Sloan, Roy, *Wings of War Over Gwynedd* (Gwasg Carreg Gwalch, 1991)

Sloan, Roy, *The Tale of Tabun* (Gwasg Carreg Gwalch, 1998)

Smith, Dai, *Aneurin Bevan and the World of South Wales* (University of Wales Press, 1993)

*South Wales Evening Post, Memories of Swansea at War* (Archive Publications, 1988)

Swain, Fay, *Wales and the Second World War – Women* (Mid Glamorgan County Council, 1989)

Tapper, Philip, *Wales and the Second World War – Voices* (Mid Glamorgan County Council, 1989)

Tapper, Philip and Susan Hawthorne, *Wales and the Second World War* (Mid Glamorgan County Council, 1991)

Taylor, Warwick, *The Forgotten Conscripts* (The Pentland Press, 2003)

Tipton, John, *Tenby During World War Two* (Tenby Museum, 1986)

Verrill-Rhys, Leigh and Deidre Beddoe (Eds.), *Parachutes and Petticoats, Welsh Women Writing on the Second World War* (Honno, 1994)

Thomas, Donald, *The Underground at War* (John Murray, 2003)

Williams, Gwyn A., *Fishers of Men* (Gomer Press, 1996)

Williams, Herbert, *Come Out Wherever You Are: The Great Escape in Wales* (Gomer Press)

Williams, Mari A., *A Forgotten Army* (University of Wales Press, 2002)

Williams, Mari A., 'In the Wars 1914–1945' from *The People of Wales*, eds. Dai Smith and Gareth Elwyn Jones (Gomer, 1999)

The following websites are useful sources of information:

BBC – WW2 People's War – written by the public, gathered by the BBC.

Gathering the Jewels: the website for Welsh heritage and culture.

The National Library of Wales – www.abandonedcommunities.co.uk (for information on Mynydd Epynt).

# Index